TENNESSEE RULES OF EVIDENCE 2021

Complete Rules in Effect as of March 1, 2021

This 2021 edition of the Tennessee Rules of Evidence provides the practitioner with a convenient copy to bring to court or the office. Also contains Advisory Commission Comments. Look for other titles such as the Tennessee Rules of Civil Procedure 2021.

ISBN: 9798717356817

Peter Edwards, Esq.
Tennessee Legal Publishing, LLC

Table of Contents

RULE 101: SCOPE

These rules shall govern evidence rulings in all trial courts of Tennessee except as otherwise provided by statute or rules of the Supreme Court of Tennessee.

Advisory Commission Comments.
These rules would apply in all trials, including those in general sessions courts and juvenile courts. See T.R.Juv.P. 28(c) (adjudicatory hearings). Sentencing proceedings are not covered, with respect to strict application of the hearsay exclusionary rule. See T.C.A. § 40-35-209(b), T.C.A. § 39-2-203(c), and T.R.Juv.P. 32(f). Administrative hearings are not covered. See T.C.A. § 4-5-313(1).

Advisory Commission Comments [1991].
The Tennessee Claims Commission applies the Tennessee Rules of Evidence by incorporation through internal Rule 43.

Advisory Commission Comments [1993].
These rules apply in all trials, including those in general sessions and juvenile courts. Some hearings, however, are not controlled solely by these rules. Preliminary proceedings and sentencing proceedings often involve hearsay not admissible under traditional exceptions. See, for example, T.C.A. § 40-35-209(b) and T.R.Juv.P. 15(b), 16(a), and 32(f). Administrative hearings are not governed exclusively by these rules; see T.C.A. § 4-5-313(1). The Tennessee Claims Commission, on the other hand, incorporates the Tennessee Rules of Evidence through internal Rule 43.

RULE 102: PURPOSE AND CONSTRUCTION

These rules shall be construed to secure the just, speedy, and inexpensive determination of proceedings.

Advisory Commission Comments.
This language comes from T.R.Civ.P. 1.

RULE 103: RULINGS ON EVIDENCE.

(a) Effect of Erroneous Ruling. Error may not be predicated upon a ruling which admits or excludes evidence unless a substantial right of the party is affected, and

(1) *Objection.* In case the ruling is one admitting evidence, a timely objection or motion to strike appears of record, stating the specific ground of objection if the specific ground was not apparent from the context; or

(2) *Offer of Proof.* In case the ruling is one excluding evidence, the substance of the evidence and the specific evidentiary basis supporting admission were made known to the court by offer or were apparent from the context. Once the court makes a definitive ruling on the record admitting or excluding evidence, either at or before trial, a party need not renew an objection or offer of proof to preserve a claim of error for appeal.

(b) Record of Offer and Ruling. The court may add any other or further statement which shows the character of the evidence, the form in which it was offered, the objection made, and the ruling.

It shall permit the making of an offer in question and answer form. If an issue arises concerning the privileged nature of a communication, the trial court may require the communication be reduced to writing for in camera review. If ruled not privileged, the communication can be divulged in open court and will become part of the record for appellate review. If ruled privileged, the trial court shall seal the writing reviewed in camera and attach it to the record for appellate review.

(c) Hearing of Jury. In jury cases, proceedings shall be conducted to the extent practicable so as to prevent inadmissible evidence from being suggested to the jury by any means, such as making statements or offers of proof or asking questions in the hearing of the jury.

(d) Plain Error. Nothing in this rule precludes taking notice of plain errors affecting substantial rights although they were not brought to the attention of the court. [As amended by order entered January 25, 1991, effective July 1, 1991; by order filed January 23, 2001, effective July 1, 2001; and by order filed January 6, 2005, effective July 1, 2005.]

Advisory Commission Comments.

Part (a) restates current law. Errors must be substantial rather than harmless. The effect of a trial error, including an erroneous ruling on evidence, is set out if T.R.A.P. 36(b). Objections must be timely and specific. Offers of proof must indicate to the reviewing court what was excluded. Note that in Part (b) the trial court must permit a formal question-and-answer offer, the kind favored by appellate courts.

Part (d) recognizes that some errors are so plain and harmful that a trial judge can be reversed despite absence of objection. See T.R.A.P. 36(b), T.R.Crim.P. 52(b), and State v. Ogle, 666 S.W.2d 58 (Tenn. 1984) (reversing for Bruton error not raised in trial court or Court of Criminal Appeals).

Advisory Commission Comments [1991].

Subsection (a)(2) is amended to add a specificity requirement as to the evidentiary rule supporting an offer of proof, thereby making this requirement for offers consistent with that for objections in subsection (a)(1).

Advisory Commission Comments [2001].

The final sentence of Rule 103(a) eliminates the need to repeat objections or offers of proof.

Advisory Commission Comments [2005].

The second paragraph in Rule 103(b) provides a procedure for appellate review where parties disagree whether a communication is privileged. Rulings at trial are subject to interlocutory appeals pursuant to Appellate Rules 9 and 10.

RULE 104: PRELIMINARY QUESTIONS

(a) Questions of Admissibility Generally. Preliminary questions concerning the qualification of a person to be a witness, the existence of a privilege, or the admissibility of evidence shall be determined by the court, subject to the provisions of subdivision (b). In making its determination the court is not bound by the rules of evidence except those with respect to privileges.

(b) Relevance Conditioned on Fact. When the relevance of evidence depends on the fulfillment of a condition of fact, the court shall admit it upon the introduction of evidence sufficient to support a finding of the fulfillment of the condition. In the court's discretion, evidence may be admitted subject to subsequent introduction of evidence sufficient to support a finding of the fulfillment of the condition.

(c) Hearing of Jury. Hearings on the admissibility of confessions shall in all cases be conducted out of the hearing of the jury. Hearings on other preliminary matters shall be so conducted when the interests of justice require or when an accused is a witness and so requests.

(d) Testimony of Accused. The accused does not by testifying upon a preliminary matter become subject to cross-examination as to other issues in the case.

(e) Weight and Credibility. This rule does not limit the right of a party to introduce before the jury evidence relevant to weight or credibility.

[As amended by order entered January 25, 1991, effective July 1, 1991.]

<u>Advisory Commission Comments.</u>

Part (a) governs the fact questions to be resolved by trial courts in deciding whether a sufficient foundation has been laid. For example, the court must decide that the declarant believed death was imminent in order to admit a dying declaration. This preliminary determination can be based on hearsay, because the judge should be able to separate reliable from unreliable proof.

Part (b) allows the court to admit evidence over a relevancy objection on condition that the offering party prove other facts making the evidence relevant. If subsequent proof fails to establish relevancy, the conditionally admitted evidence should be stricken with an appropriate jury instruction; extreme prejudice could result in a mistrial.

Whether preliminary questions are determined outside the jury's presence is discretionary under Part (c), except where a confession is offered or where the accused in a criminal case is a witness and requests a jury-out hearing through counsel.

RULE 105: LIMITED ADMISSIBILITY

When evidence which is admissible as to one party or for one purpose but not admissible as to another party or for another purpose is admitted, the court upon request shall restrict the evidence to its proper scope and instruct the jury accordingly.

<u>Advisory Commission Comments.</u>

This is the common law rule.

RULE 106: WRITINGS OR RECORDED STATEMENTS — COMPLETENESS.

When a writing or recorded statement or part thereof is introduced by a party, an adverse party may require the introduction at that time of any other part or any other writing or recorded statement which ought in fairness to be considered contemporaneously with it.

<u>Advisory Commission Comments.</u>

The rule restates settled law.

RULE 201: JUDICIAL NOTICE OF ADJUDICATIVE FACTS.

(a) Scope of Rule - This rule governs only judicial notice of adjudicative facts.

(b) Kinds of Facts - A judicially noticed fact must be one not subject to reasonable dispute, in that it is either (1) generally known within the territorial jurisdiction of the trial court or (2) capable of accurate and ready determination by resort to sources whose accuracy cannot reasonably be questioned.

(c) When Discretionary - A court may take judicial notice whether requested or not.

(d) When Mandatory - A court shall take judicial notice if requested by a party and supplied with the necessary information.

(e) Opportunity to Be Heard - A party is entitled upon timely request to an opportunity to be heard as to the propriety of taking judicial notice and the tenor of the matter noticed. In the absence of prior notification, the request may be made after judicial notice is taken.

(f) Time of Taking Notice - Judicial notice may be taken at any stage of the proceeding.

(g) Instructing the Jury - In a civil action or proceeding, the court shall instruct the jury to accept as conclusive any fact judicially noticed. In a criminal case, the court shall instruct the jury that it may, but is not required to, accept as conclusive any fact judicially noticed.

<u>Advisory Commission Comments.</u>

Judicial notice really does not involve admission and exclusion of evidence; rather, no evidence is necessary. Part (b) limits judicial notice to a relatively small class of adjudicative facts. The lawyer may have to supply the court with reference materials, such as an almanac.

RULE 202: JUDICIAL NOTICE OF LAW.

(a) Mandatory Judicial Notice of Law. The court shall take judicial notice of (1) the common law, (2) the constitutions and statutes of the United States and of every state, territory, and other jurisdiction of the United States, (3) all rules adopted by the United States Supreme Court or by the Tennessee Supreme Court, and (4) any rule or regulation of which a statute of the United States or Tennessee mandates judicial notice.

(b) Optional Judicial Notice of Law. Upon reasonable notice to adverse parties, a party may request that the court take, and the court may take, judicial notice of (1) all other duly adopted federal and state rules of court, (2) all duly published regulations of federal and state agencies and proclamations of the Tennessee Wildlife Resources Agency, (3) all duly enacted ordinances of municipalities or other governmental subdivisions, (4) any matter of law which would fall within the scope of this subsection or subsection (a) of this rule but for the fact that it has been replaced, superseded, or otherwise rendered no longer in force, and (5) treaties, conventions, the laws of foreign countries, international law, and maritime law.

(c) Determination by Court. All determinations of law made pursuant to this rule shall be made by the court and not by the jury. In making its determination the court is not bound by the rules of evidence except those with respect to privileges.

[As amended by order entered January 25, 1991, effective July 1, 1991.]

<u>Advisory Commission Comments.</u>

Note that judicial notice of ordinances is discretionary and requires notice to adverse parties.
See also the Uniform Judicial Notice Act, T.C.A. § 24-6-201 —207 [§§ 24-6-201 —24-6-206
repealed].

Advisory Commission Comments [1991].
The Tennessee Wildlife Resources Agency issues proclamations to regulate hunting seasons and
limits. These are published in the Administrative Register. Under the amended rule, a court could
judicially notice such proclamations.

Article III. Presumptions

RULE 301: RESERVED

Advisory Commission Comments. The Commission believed that presumptions were outside the scope of its present assignment from the Tennessee Supreme Court.

RULE 401: DEFINITION OF "RELEVANT EVIDENCE."

"Relevant evidence" means evidence having any tendency to make the existence of any fact that is of consequence to the determination of the action more probable or less probable than it would be without the evidence.

Advisory Commission Comments.
This proposal does not change Tennessee common law. The theoretical test for admissibility is a lenient one, as it should be, and practical difficulties can be resolved under Rule 403 or the exclusionary rules of legal relevancy that follow.
The materiality concept is found in the words, "any fact that is of consequence to the determination of the action."To be relevant, evidence must tend to prove a material issue.

RULE 402: RELEVANT EVIDENCE GENERALLY ADMISSIBLE; IRRELEVANT EVIDENCE INADMISSIBLE.

All relevant evidence is admissible except as provided by the Constitution of the United States, the Constitution of Tennessee, these rules, or other rules or laws of general application in the courts of Tennessee. Evidence which is not relevant is not admissible.

Advisory Commission Comments.
Once evidence satisfies the definition of relevance, it becomes admissible unless a rule excludes it.

RULE 403: EXCLUSION OF RELEVANT EVIDENCE ON GROUNDS OF PREJUDICE, CONFUSION, OR WASTE OF TIME.

Although relevant, evidence may be excluded if its probative value is substantially outweighed by the danger of unfair prejudice, confusion of the issues, or misleading the jury, or by considerations of undue delay, waste of time, or needless presentation of cumulative evidence.

Advisory Commission Comments.
The Tennessee Supreme Court approved this rule for both civil and criminal cases in *State v. Banks*, 564 S.W.2d 947 (Tenn. 1978).

RULE 404: CHARACTER EVIDENCE NOT ADMISSIBLE TO PROVE CONDUCT; EXCEPTIONS; OTHER CRIMES.

(a) Character Evidence Generally. Evidence of a person's character or trait of character is not admissible for the purpose of proving action in conformity therewith on a particular occasion, except:
(1) *Character of Accused.* In a criminal case, evidence of a pertinent trait of character offered by an accused or by the prosecution to rebut the same or, if evidence of a trait of character of the alleged victim of the crime is offered by the accused and admitted under Rule 404(a)(2), evidence of the same trait of character of the accused offered by the prosecution;

(2) *Character of Alleged Victim.* In a criminal case, and subject to the limitations imposed by Rule 412, evidence of a pertinent trait of character of the alleged victim of the crime offered by an accused or by the prosecution to rebut the same, or evidence of a character trait of peacefulness of the alleged victim offered by the prosecution in a homicide case to rebut evidence that the alleged victim was the first aggressor;

(3) *Character of Witness.* Evidence of the character of a witness as provided in Rules 607,608, and 609.

(b) Other Crimes, Wrongs, or Acts. Evidence of other crimes, wrongs, or acts is not admissible to prove the character of a person in order to show action in conformity with the character trait. It may, however, be admissible for other purposes. The conditions which must be satisfied before allowing such evidence are:

(1) The court upon request must hold a hearing outside the jury's presence;

(2) The court must determine that a material issue exists other than conduct conforming with a character trait and must upon request state on the record the material issue, the ruling, and the reasons for admitting the evidence;

(3) The court must find proof of the other crime, wrong, or act to be clear and convincing; and

(4) The court must exclude the evidence if its probative value is outweighed by the danger of unfair prejudice.

[As amended by order filed January 31, 2003, effective July 1, 2003; and by order filed January 8, 2009, effective July 1, 2009.]

<u>Advisory Commission Comments.</u>

Part (a) has always been the law in Tennessee for criminal prosecutions.

T.C.A. § 40-17-119 [repealed; see 1991 comments] regulates character evidence offered to prove a rape victim's alleged consent.

In civil actions, Tennessee is one of a minority of jurisdictions admitting character evidence in some situations to prove circumstantially conduct involving "moral turpitude." *Spears & Solomon v. International Insurance Co.*, 60 Tenn. 370 (1872). The proposed rule would change that minority position; character would be inadmissible circumstantially in all civil cases. Of course, if character is directly at issue in a civil action, such as in a defamation action, character evidence necessarily is relevant and admissible under Rule 405(b).

The Commission drafted Part (b) in accord with the Supreme Court's pronouncements in *State v. Parton*, 694 S.W.2d 299 (Tenn. 1985). There the Court established precise procedures to emphasize that evidence of other crimes should usually be excluded. In the exceptional case where another crime is arguably relevant to an issue other than the accused's character —issues such as identity (including motive and common scheme or plan), intent, or rebuttal of accident or mistake —the trial judge must first excuse the jury. Then the judge must decide what material issue other than character forms a proper basis for relevancy. If the objecting party requests, the trial judge must state on the record the issue, the ruling, and the reason for ruling the evidence admissible. Finally, the judge must always weigh in the balance probative value and unfair prejudice. If the danger of unfair prejudice outweighs the probative value, the court should exclude the evidence even though it bears on a material issue aside from character. Finally, according to *Parton*, the trial judge must find that the evidence is "clear and convincing" that the defendant committed another crime.

<u>Advisory Commission Comments [1991].</u>

[In place of the second paragraph of earlier language, which is rescinded, insert the following language as the new second paragraph:]
The character of the victim of a sex crime is not governed by Rule 404(a)(2), but rather by T.R.Evid. 412.

Advisory Commission Comment [2003].
The third condition for admitting other crimes, clear and convincing proof, has been required by case law before and after adoption of the Rules of Evidence. This principle was first enunciated in *Wrather v. State*, 179 Tenn. 666 (1943), reversing a mother's conviction for murdering her adult son by arsenic poisoning. Evidence that she killed her father-in-law and brother-in-law with arsenic was not clear and convincing. The Supreme Court again approved this standard in *State v. Parton*, 694 S.W.2d 299 (1985).

Advisory Commission Comment [2005].
The word "person" in Rule 404(b) has been construed to refer solely to the defendant in a criminal prosecution. *State v. Stevens*, 78 S.W.3d 817 (Tenn. 2002).

Advisory Commission Comment [2009].
If the accused attacks the character of the alleged victim, amended Rule 404(a)(1) allows the prosecution to prove the accused's character for the same trait. This is an additional way the accused "opens the door" to character evidence.

RULE 405: METHODS OF PROVING CHARACTER.

(a) Reputation or Opinion. In all cases in which evidence of character or a trait of character of a person is admissible, proof may be made by testimony as to reputation or by testimony in the form of an opinion. After application to the court, inquiry on cross-examination is allowable into relevant specific instances of conduct. The conditions which must be satisfied before allowing inquiry on cross-examination about specific instances of conduct are:
(1) The court upon request must hold a hearing outside the jury's presence,
(2) The court must determine that a reasonable factual basis exists for the inquiry, and

(3) The court must determine that the probative value of a specific instance of conduct on the character witness's credibility outweighs its prejudicial effect on substantive issues.

(b) Specific Instances of Conduct. In cases in which character or a trait of character of a person is an essential element of a charge, claim, or defense, proof may also be made of specific instances of that person's conduct.

Advisory Commission Comments.
This rule changes Tennessee law, which does not permit character to be proved by personal opinion.

Cross-examination of character witnesses for the accused raises a delicate problem. The examining lawyer can ask the witness about rumored arrests and charges concerning the defendant, because the witness's knowledge of the rumors might impeach the witness in the eyes of the jurors. If the witness admits having heard unfavorable rumors, the jury may decide that the witness's reputation or opinion testimony is entitled to little weight. If the witness has not heard the rumors, the witness's testimony may likewise be taken with a grain of salt because the witness is unfamiliar with the accused or the accused's community.

The indirect effect of such a cross-examination may be the more damaging to the accused. While the jury will be instructed to consider the rumors only as affecting the character witness's credibility, the practical danger is that such rumors - even if untrue - place the defendant's character in a bad light with the jurors. In an effort to alleviate the problem, the proposed rule sets out detailed procedural safeguards. The cross-examiner must apply to the court for permission to inquire into specific instances of conduct, the jury must be excused, and the court must determine both that a factual basis exists and that probative value for impeachment outweighs prejudicial effect on the accused's character.

Part (b) allows substantive proof of specific acts where the character is an element of a cause of action or a defense. For instance, the defendant who called a defamed plaintiff a "crook" can prove the plaintiff embezzled funds.

RULE 406: HABIT; ROUTINE PRACTICE.

(a) Evidence of the habit of a person, an animal, or of the routine practice of an organization, whether corroborated or not and regardless of the presence of eye-witnesses, is relevant to prove that the conduct of the person, animal, or organization on a particular occasion was in conformity with the habit or routine practice.

(b) A habit is a regular response to a repeated specific situation. A routine practice is a regular course of conduct of an organization.

Advisory Commission Comments.

Tennessee has long admitted animal habit. *Copley v. State*, 153 Tenn. 189, 281 S.W. 460 (1925), is the leading case. Authorities supporting admissibility of human habit and business custom are collected in Tennessee Law of Evidence § 30.

The second paragraph defines habit and routine practice, emphasizing the need for a "regular response" when a person, animal, or organization is faced with a given situation.

RULE 407: SUBSEQUENT REMEDIAL MEASURES.

When, after an event, measures are taken which, if taken previously, would have made the event less likely to occur, evidence of the subsequent remedial measures is not admissible to prove strict liability, negligence, or culpable conduct in connection with the event. This rule does not require the exclusion of evidence of subsequent measures when offered for another purpose, such as proving controverted ownership, control, or feasibility of precautionary measures, or impeachment.

Advisory Commission Comments.
This rule and current Tennessee law exclude subsequent measures to remedy defects to prove negligence or culpable conduct. *Illinois Central Railroad Co. v. Wyatt,* 104 Tenn. 432, 58 S.W. 308 (1900). The rule adds, however, a specific exclusion in strict liability actions as well. Such is the majority federal view, including that of the Sixth Circuit. See *Hall v. American Steamship Co.,* 688 F.2d 1062 (6th Cir. 1982) (admiralty). Manufacturers should be encouraged to improve product designs without fear of encountering damaging evidence.

A defendant who controverts ownership, control, or feasibility opens the door for the plaintiff to introduce subsequent remedial measures. Similarly, an expert who opines that a design could not be improved upon invites attack by the impeachment exception to this otherwise exclusionary rule.

RULE 408: COMPROMISE AND OFFERS TO COMPROMISE.

Evidence of (1) furnishing or offering to furnish or (2) accepting or offering to accept a valuable consideration in compromising or attempting to compromise a claim, whether in the present litigation or related litigation, which claim was disputed or was reasonably expected to be disputed as to either validity or amount, is not admissible to prove liability for or invalidity of a civil claim or its amount or a criminal charge or its punishment. Evidence of conduct or statements made in compromise negotiations is likewise not admissible. This rule does not require the exclusion of any evidence actually obtained during discovery merely because it is presented in the course of compromise negotiations. This rule also does not require exclusion when the evidence is offered for another purpose, such as proving bias or prejudice of a witness, negativing a contention of undue delay, or proving an effort to obstruct a criminal investigation or prosecution; however, a party may not be impeached by a prior inconsistent statement made in compromise negotiations.

Advisory Commission Comments.
The rule would work only slight changes in Tennessee evidence law. One difference is that statements of fact during settlement negotiations become inadmissible, but that is an improvement over the present practice admitting the fact statements.
Also salutary is the provision excluding compromises and settlement offers in "related litigation."The drafted language would change the suggestion to the contrary in T*ennessee Coach Co. v. Young*, 18 Tenn. App. 592, 80 S.W.2d 107 (1934). Consistent with the proposal is T.C.A. § 29-11-105(b), excluding evidence of settlement by one tortfeasor where another goes to trial.
Tennessee courts exclude settlements and settlement offers only in civil trials, admitting them in criminal prosecutions. *Carter v. State*, 161 Tenn. 698, 34 S.W.2d 208 (1931). The proposed rule excludes such evidence in both civil and criminal trials.

Advisory Commission Comments [1993].
Where punitive damages are at issue, compromise offers become relevant and admissible despite Rule 408. See *Hodges v. S.C. Toof & Company*, 833 S.W.2d 896 (Tenn. 1992).

RULE 409.1: EXPRESSIONS OF SYMPATHY OR BENEVOLENCE.

(a) That portion of statements, writings, or benevolent gestures expressing sympathy or a general sense of benevolence relating to the pain, suffering or death of a person involved in an accident and made to such person or to the family of such person shall be inadmissible as evidence of an admission of liability in a civil action. A statement of fault that is part of, or in addition to, any of the above shall not be inadmissible because of this Rule.

(b) For purposes of this Rule:

(1) "Accident" means an occurrence resulting in injury or death to one or more persons which is not the result of willful action by a party.

(2) "Benevolent gestures" means actions which convey a sense of compassion or commiseration emanating from humane impulses.

(3) "Family" means an injured party's spouse, parent, grandparent, stepparent, child, grandchild, sibling, half sibling, adopted sibling, or parent-in-law.

[Added by order filed January 31, 2003, effective July 1, 2003.]

<u>Advisory Commission Comment [2003].</u>

Rule 409.1 renders inadmissible certain statements and actions reflecting sympathy for persons injured in accidents. This Rule, like Evidence Rules 408, 409, and 410, is designed to encourage the settlement of lawsuits. It complements Evidence Rule 409, which makes inadmissible payment of medical and related expenses on the issue of liability. The underlying theory of Rule 409.1 is that a settlement of a lawsuit is more likely if the defendant is free to express sympathy for the plaintiff's injuries without making a statement that would be admissible as an admission of a party opponent. Without this rule, a defendant's statement such is "I am sorry that you have suffered so much from the accident" might well be admissible as an admission of a party opponent. Accordingly, defense counsel may advise against making such statements in order to avoid the creation of harmful evidence. Yet a simple apology may go a long way toward making an injured party feel more comfortable with a nonjudicial settlement of the matter. This process is consistent with the modern focus on mediation and other methods of dispute resolution that seek to avoid a trial by facilitating a resolution acceptable to all parties.

The rule is similar to that enacted in Massachusetts (Mass Ann. Laws ch. 233, § 23D) and California (West's Ann. Cal. Evid.Code § 1160). A Texas provision is also consistent with Rule 409.1. See Vernon's Tex. Stat. & Code Ann., Civ. Prac. & Remedies Code §18.061.

Rule 409.1 embraces only civil cases involving an "accident." It is inapplicable in criminal cases. It also extends only to "benevolent gestures"; it does not exclude statements of fault.

RULE 409: PAYMENT OF MEDICAL AND SIMILAR EXPENSES.

Evidence of furnishing or offering or promising to pay medical, hospital, or similar expenses occasioned by an injury is not admissible to prove liability for the injury.

<u>Advisory Commission Comments.</u>

The rule and the Tennessee case law are the same. *Meegal v. Memphis Street Railway Co.*, 33 Tenn. App. 247, 238 S.W.2d 519 (1950). The rule applies to civil, not criminal, trials.

Except as otherwise provided in this rule, evidence of the following is not, in any civil or criminal proceeding, admissible against the party who made the plea or was a participant in the plea discussions:

(1) A plea of guilty which was later withdrawn;

(2) A plea of nolo contendere;

(3) Any statement made in the course of any proceedings under Rule 11 of the Tennessee Rules of Criminal Procedure regarding either of the foregoing pleas; or

(4) Any statement made in the course of plea discussions with an attorney for the prosecuting authority which do not result in a plea of guilty or which result in a plea of guilty later withdrawn. Such a statement is admissible, however, in a criminal proceeding for perjury or false statement if the statement was made by the defendant under oath, on the record, and in the presence of counsel.

<u>Advisory Commission Comments.</u>
This rule is cross-referenced in T.R.Crim.P. 11(d).

<u>Advisory Commission Comments [1994].</u>

Williams v. Brown, 860 S.W.2d 854 (Tenn. 1993), held misdemeanor traffic fine payments without court appearance inadmissible by analogy to Rule 410.

<u>Advisory Commission Comments [2013].</u>

The original Advisory Commission Comment wa revised to correct an obsolete cross-reference to a now nonexistent subparagraph of Tenn. R. Crim. P 11.

Evidence that a person was or was not insured against liability is not admissible upon issues of negligence or other wrongful conduct. This rule does not require the exclusion of evidence of insurance against liability when offered for another purpose, such as proof of agency, ownership, or control, or bias or prejudice of a witness.

<u>Advisory Commission Comments.</u>
The rule restates Tennessee common law.

Notwithstanding any other provision of law, in a criminal trial, preliminary hearing, deposition, or other proceeding in which a person is accused of an offense under Tenn. Code Ann. §39-13-309 [trafficking a person for a commercial sex act], § 39-13-502 [aggravated rape], §39-13-503 [rape], §39-13-504 [aggravated sexual battery], §39-13-505 [sexual battery], §39-13-506 [statutory rape], §39-13-507 [spousal sexual offenses], §39-13-509 [sexual contact by minor with an authority figure], §39-13-522 [rape of a child], §39-13-527 [sexual battery by an authority figure], Tenn. Code Ann. §39-13-528 [solicitation of minors for sexual acts], §39-13-531 [aggrivated rape of a child], §35-13-532 [statutory rape by an authority figure], §39-13-533 [promoting travel for prostitution], §39-15-302 [incest] or the attempt to commit any such offense, the following rules apply:

(a) Definition of sexual behavior. In this rule "sexual behavior" means sexual activity of the alleged victim other than the sexual act at issue in the case.

(b) Reputation or opinion. Reputation or opinion evidence of the sexual behavior of an alleged victim of such offense is inadmissible unless admitted in accordance with the procedures in subdivision (d) of this Rule and required by the Tennessee or United States Constitution.

(c) Specific instances of conduct. Evidence of specific instances of a victim's sexual behavior is inadmissible unless admitted in accordance with the procedures in subdivision (d) of this rule, and the evidence is:

(1) Required by the Tennessee or United States Constitution, or

(2) Offered by the defendant on the issue of credibility of the victim, provided the prosecutor or victim has presented evidence as to the victim's sexual behavior, and only to the extent needed to rebut the specific evidence presented by the prosecutor or victim, or

(3) If the sexual behavior was with the accused, on the issue of consent, or

(4) If the sexual behavior was with persons other than the accused,

(i) to rebut or explain scientific or medical evidence, or

(ii) to prove or explain the source of semen, injury, disease, or knowledge of sexual matters, or

(iii) to prove consent if the evidence is of a pattern of sexual behavior so distinctive and so closely resembling the accused's version of the alleged encounter with the victim that it tends to prove that the victim consented to the act charged or behaved in such a manner as to lead the defendant reasonably to believe that the victim consented.

(d) Procedures. If a person accused of an offense covered by this Rule intends to offer under subdivision (b) reputation or opinion evidence or under subdivision (c) specific instances of conduct of the victim, the following procedures apply:

(1) the person must file a written motion to offer such evidence.

(i) The motion shall be filed no later than ten days before the date on which the trial is scheduled to begin, except the court may allow the motion to be made at a later date, including during trial, if the court determines either that the evidence is newly discovered and could not have been obtained earlier through the exercise of due diligence or that the issue to which the evidence relates has newly arisen in the case.

(ii) The motion shall be served on all parties, the prosecuting attorney, and the victim; Service on the victim shall be made through the prosecuting attorney's office.

(iii) The motion shall be accompanied by a written offer of proof, describing the specific evidence and the purpose for introducing it.

(2) When a motion required by subdivision (d)(1) is filed and found by the court to comply with the requirements of this rule, the court shall hold a hearing in chambers or otherwise out of the hearing of the public and the jury to determine whether the evidence described in the motion is admissible. The hearing shall be on the record, but the record shall be sealed except for the limited purposes of facilitating appellate review, assisting the court or parties in their preparation of the case, and to impeach under subdivision (d)(3)(iii).

(3) At this hearing

(i) The victim may attend in person,

(ii) The parties may call witnesses, including the alleged victim, and offer relevant evidence, and

(iii) the accused may testify but the testimony during this hearing may not be used against the accused in the preliminary hearing, trial, or other proceeding, except that such testimony may be admissible to impeach the credibility of the defendant if the defendant elects to testify at the preliminary hearing, trial, or other proceeding.

(4) If the court determines that the evidence which the accused seeks to offer satisfies subdivisions (b) or (c) and that the probative value of the evidence outweighs its unfair prejudice to the victim, the evidence shall be admissible in the proceeding to the extent an order made by the court specifies the evidence which may be offered and areas with respect to which the alleged victim may be examined or cross-examined.

[As added by order entered January 25, 1991, effective July 1, 1991; amended by order entered January 26, 1999, effective July 1, 1999 and as amended by order filed January 8, 2019 effective October 1, 2019.]

Advisory Commission Comments [1991].

This rule governs the admissibility of evidence of a sex crime victim's sexual history in cases involving the sex crimes specified in the first sentence of the rule. It replaces the current rape-shield statute, T.C.A. § 40-17-119 [repealed], and is to be applied in lieu of Tennessee Rule of Evidence 404(a)(2) (character of crime victim) for the specified sex crimes. Like T.C.A. § 40-17-119 [repealed] and Federal Rule of Evidence 412, this rule strikes a balance between the paramount interests of the accused in a fair trial and the important interests of the sexual assault victim in avoiding an unnecessary, degrading, and embarrassing invasion of sexual privacy. Rule 412 recognizes the important interests of all involved —the victim, the public, and the criminal accused —and provides standards and procedures to assist courts in determining when such evidence is admissible. It specifically recognizes that, despite the embarrassing nature of the proof, sometimes the accused can only have a fair trial if permitted to introduce evidence of the alleged victim's sexual history. On the other hand, the rule also takes into account that the public's interest in prosecuting and convicting people guilty of various sexual offenses is frustrated when sexual assault victims refuse to report the offenses or to testify about them at trial because of the possible admission of evidence of their sexual history. Moreover, the rule seeks to minimize the likelihood that evidence of the alleged victim's sexual history may cause the jury to be unfairly prejudiced against the victim.

This rule is much more comprehensive than T.C.A. § 40-17-119 [repealed], which deals only with proof of specific instances of a sexual assault victim's sexual behavior with third persons and only when that evidence is to be used on the issue of consent. T.C.A. § 40-17-119 [repealed] does not address difficult questions of the admissibility of reputation and opinion evidence, of evidence of prior sexual activity with the accused, or of proof in sexual assault cases on issues other than consent. The narrow focus of this statute has resulted in Tennessee case law questioning its constitutionality in certain applications. See *Shockley v. State*, 585 S.W.2d 645 (Tenn. Crim. App. 1978).

Rule 412 deals with three types of proof: reputation, opinion, and specific acts. Subdivision (b) limits the use of reputation and opinion evidence about the victim's sexual behavior. Because such evidence is embarrassing and seldom probative, it is admissible only in those unusual cases where the United States or Tennessee Constitution mandates admissibility. *Cf. Doe v. United States*, 666 F.2d 43 (4th Cir. 1981) (recognizes possibility that constitution could require admission of reputation and opinion evidence in extraordinary circumstances). When such evidence is admissible, the procedures outlined in subdivision (d) must be followed.

Subdivision (c) tells when specific acts of the victim's sexual history may be admissible if the procedures in subdivision (d) are satisfied. Because of the infinite variety of factual situations that can arise in sex crime cases, no evidence rule can detail all the possible situations where evidence of sexual history is required by the accused's Due Process rights. Subdivision (c)(1) recognizes this and provides that specific acts are admissible when required by the United States or Tennessee Constitution. *Cf. State v. Jalo*, 27 Or. App. 845, 557 P.2d 1359 (1976) (criminal accused's confrontation rights entitle him to prove that rape victim charged him with crime to retaliate for his discovery of her sexual relations with his son); *Commonwealth v. Black*, 337 Pa. Super. 548, 487 A.2d 396 (1985) (confrontation clause permits criminal accused to prove sex crime victim's bias; she allegedly reported crime so she could remove him from house in order to continue sexual relations with another house member and to punish him for interfering with this sexual relationship).

Subdivision (c)(2) provides that specific instances of the victim's sexual behavior may also be admissible to rebut evidence presented by the prosecution about the victim's sexual behavior. This exception is narrow, however. It only permits the defendant to prove specific acts when needed to rebut the specific evidence presented by the prosecution's proof. It does not open the door to the victim's entire sexual history.

Subdivision (c)(3) indicates that the victim's sexual behavior with the accused may be admissible on the issue of consent. If consent is not an issue, this subdivision does not apply.

Subdivision (c)(4) lists three situations where the victim's sexual behavior with persons other than the accused may be admissible. First, the proof may be used to rebut or explain scientific or medical evidence. Second, it may be used to prove or explain the source of semen, injury, or disease. For example, the defendant may prove that the victim, who testified that he or she contracted the AIDS virus from the defendant, actually contracted it from a named third party. Similarly, if it is alleged that the defendant's illegal sexual activity caused the victim to become pregnant, the defendant may prove that the victim had sexual relations with a third party who fathered the child. See *Shockley v. State,* 585 S.W.2d 645 (Tenn. Crim. App. 1978) (rape defendant entitled to prove someone else caused victim's pregnancy). This provision also permits proof of the source of knowledge of sexual matters. It will most frequently be used in cases where the victim is a young child who testifies in detail about sexual activity. To disprove any suggestion that the child acquired the detailed information about sexual matters from the encounter with the accused, the defense may want to prove that the child learned the terminology as the result of sexual activity with third parties. Third, the defendant may prove acts with third parties in the so-called "signature" cases to prove consent. These acts are so similar to the defendant's version of the offense that they corroborate the defendant's story.

In order to ensure that the victim's privacy is not inappropriately compromised when the court assesses whether a given item of evidence is admissible under the rule, subdivision (d), like T.C.A. § 40-17-119 [repealed], provides specific procedures that must be followed before evidence is admitted under this rule. First, subdivision (d)(1) requires the defendant to file a written motion of an intent to offer evidence covered by the rule. The motion shall be filed 10 days before the trial unless the exceptions mentioned in the rule apply. The ten day rule is designed to provide the prosecution and the victim an opportunity to investigate the proposed proof and to contest the issue. The motion is to be served on all parties, the prosecuting attorney, and the victim. To facilitate preparation, the motion must describe both the evidence to be offered and the purpose for offering it.

If a motion is filed and the court determines that the evidence is the kind of evidence possibly covered by the rule, it should hold a hearing, pursuant to subdivision (d)(2). The victim's privacy is somewhat protected since the proceeding must be held outside the hearing of the public. The rule specifically provides that the hearing may be held in chambers. The hearing must be on the record to permit appellate review, but the record of the hearing is sealed.

Subdivision (d)(3) indicates that the victim has a right to attend the hearing and that all parties may call witnesses and offer evidence on the issue whether the proof of the victim's sexual behavior should be introduced.

In order to protect the defendant's right to remain silent, the defendant may testify at his hearing without producing evidence admissible as substantive evidence at the trial. The defendant's testimony at the hearing may, however, be used to impeach the defendant at the later trial.

After the hearing the court must balance the evidence's probative value against the harm that disclosure will cause to the victim. This balance includes consideration of the harmful effect the proof may have on the victim. If the probative value outweighs the listed factors and the evidence is admitted, the court should issue an order specifying exactly which proof will be received and which issues may be explored during questioning.

<u>Advisory Commission Comments [1996].</u>

While Rule 412 applies only to criminal prosecutions, a statute shields the civil plaintiff's sexual behavior in actions for sexual misconduct of therapists against patients. T.C.A. § 29-26-207 states that the victim's sexual history is not admissible as evidence except to prove that the sexual behavior occurred with the therapist prior to the provision of therapy to the patient by the therapist.

Advisory Commission Comments [1999].

The amendment adds other sex offenses.

Advisory Commission Comments [2019].

The 2019 amendment adds five offenses to which this rule applies and reorders the listing to the order of appearnce in the code.

RULE 501: PRIVILEGES RECOGNIZED ONLY AS PROVIDED.

Except as otherwise provided by constitution, statute, common law, or by these or other rules promulgated by the Tennessee Supreme Court, no person has a privilege to:

(1) Refuse to be a witness;

(2) Refuse to disclose any matter;

(3) Refuse to produce any object or writing; or

(4) Prevent another from being a witness or disclosing any matter or producing any object or writing.

[As amended by order filed December 14, 2009, effective July 1, 2010.]

Advisory Commission Comments [1999].

The following statutes and rules deal with some Tennessee privileges. They are provided for the convenience of the bench and bar. The relevant statutes and rules should be consulted to ensure accuracy and completeness. Many other statutes make certain documents confidential, but the Commission did not view such confidentiality concepts as synonymous with privilege theories.

T.C.A. § 55-10-114(b). ACCIDENT REPORT PRIVILEGE

 No report or information mentioned in this section [accident report made by "any person or by garages"] shall be used as evidence in any trial, civil or criminal, arising out of an accident, except that the department [of safety] shall furnish upon demand of any party to such trial, or upon demand of any court, a certificate showing that a specified accident report has or has not been made to the department in compliance with law.

T.C.A. § 55-12-128. SAME, CIVIL SUITS

 Neither the reports required by this chapter [operator's report of financial responsibility], the action taken by the commissioner pursuant to this chapter, the findings of the commissioner upon which such action is based, nor the security filed as provided in this chapter shall be referred to in any way, nor constitute any evidence of the negligence or due care of either party at the trial of any action at law to recover damages.

T.C.A. § 62-1-116. ACCOUNTANT-CLIENT PRIVILEGE

 (a) Licensees shall not divulge, nor shall they in any manner be required to divulge, any information which is communicated to them or obtained by them by the reason of the confidential nature of their employment. Such information shall be deemed confidential; provided, that nothing herein shall be construed as prohibiting the disclosure of information required to be disclosed by the standards of the public accounting profession in reporting on the examination of financial statements or as prohibiting disclosures in investigations or proceedings under this chapter, in ethical investigations conducted by private professional organizations, or in the course of peer reviews, or to other persons active in the organization performing services for that client on a need to know basis or to persons in the entity who need this information for the sole purpose of assuring quality control. Disclosure of confidential information pursuant to this section shall not constitute a waiver of the confidential nature of such information for any other purpose.

(b) Information derived as a result of such professional employment is deemed to be confidential, except that nothing in any section of this chapter shall be construed as modifying, changing or affecting the criminal or bankruptcy laws of this state or of the United States.

T.C.A. § 23-3-105. ATTORNEY-CLIENT PRIVILEGE

No attorney, solicitor or counselor shall be permitted, in giving testimony against a client, or person who consulted the attorney, solicitor or counselor professionally, to disclose any communication made to the attorney, solicitor or counselor as such by such person, during the pendency of the suit, before or afterwards, to the person's injury.

T.C.A. § 23-3-107. SAME

Any attorney offering to give testimony in any of the cases provided for in T.C.A. § 23-3-105 ... shall be rejected by the court, and such attorney commits a Class C misdemeanor, for which, on conviction, the attorney shall also be stricken from the rolls, if a practicing attorney.

T.C.A. § 24-1-209. ATTORNEY-PRIVATE DETECTIVE OR INVESTIGATOR PRIVILEGE

Communication between an attorney and a private detective or investigator hired by such attorney, while acting in their respective professional capacities shall be privileged communications.

T.C.A. § 37-1-614. CHILD SEXUAL ABUSE EXCEPTION TO PRIVILEGES

The privileged quality of communication between husband and wife and between any professional person and the professional person's patient or client, and any other privileged communication except that between attorney and client, as such communication relates both to the competency of the witness and to the exclusion of confidential communications, shall not apply to any situation involving known or suspected child sexual abuse and shall not constitute grounds for failure to report as required by this part [T.C.A. § 37-1-605], failure to cooperate with the department in its activities pursuant to this part [T.C.A. § 37-1-611(b)], or failure to give evidence in any judicial proceeding relating to child sexual abuse.

T.C.A. § 24-1-206. CLERGY-PENITENT PRIVILEGE

(a)(1) No minister of the gospel, no priest of the Catholic Church, no rector of the Episcopal Church, no ordained rabbi, and no regular minister of religion of any religious organization or denomination usually referred to as a church, over eighteen (18) years of age, shall be allowed or required in giving testimony as a witness in any litigation, to disclose any information communicated to that person in a confidential manner, properly entrusted to that person in that person's professional capacity, and necessary to enable that person to discharge the functions of such office according to the usual course of that person's practice or discipline, wherein such person so communicating such information about such person or another is seeking spiritual counsel and advice relative to and growing out of the information so imparted.

(2) It shall be the duty of the judge of the court wherein such litigation is pending, when such testimony as prohibited in this section is offered, to determine whether or not that person possesses the qualifications which prohibit that person from testifying to the communications sought to be proven by that person.

(b) The prohibition of this section shall not apply to cases where the communicating party, or parties, waives the right so conferred by personal appearance in open court so declaring, or by an affidavit properly sworn to by such a one or ones, before some person authorized to administer oaths, and filed with the court wherein litigation is pending.

(c) Nothing in this section shall modify or in any way change the law relative to "hearsay testimony."

(d) Any minister of the gospel, priest of the Catholic Church, rector of the Episcopal Church, ordained rabbi, and any regular minister of religion of any religious organization or denomination usually referred to as a church, who violates the provisions of this section, commits a Class C misdemeanor.

T.C.A. § 24-1-211(f). DEAF PERSON-INTERPRETER PRIVILEGE

Before a qualified interpreter will participate in any proceedings subsequent to an appointment under the provisions of this section, such interpreter shall make an oath or affirmation that such interpreter will make a true interpretation in an understandable manner to the deaf person for whom the interpreter is appointed and that such interpreter will interpret the statements of the deaf person desiring that statements be made, in the English language to the best of such interpreter's skill and judgment. The appointing authority shall provide recess periods as necessary for the interpreter when the interpreter so indicates. Any and all information that the interpreter gathers from the deaf person pertaining to any proceeding then pending shall at all times remain confidential and privileged, or on an equal basis with the attorney-client privilege, unless such deaf person desires that such information be communicated to other persons.

Tenn.S.Ct. Rule 9, § 27.1. DISCIPLINARY BOARD—COMPLAINANT PRIVILEGE

Communications to the board, hearing committee members or disciplinary counsel relating to lawyer misconduct or disability and testimony given in the proceedings shall be absolutely privileged, and no civil lawsuit predicated thereon may be instituted against any complainant or witnesses. Members of the board, hearing committee members, disciplinary counsel and staff shall be immune from civil suit for any conduct in the course of their official duties.

T.C.A. § 24-7-114. LEGISLATIVE COMMITTEE-WITNESS PRIVILEGE

From and after February 20, 1959, without the consent of such witness there shall not be admitted into evidence in any civil proceeding in the courts of this state the testimony of a witness given before any committee of the general assembly of the State of Tennessee, provided such testimony when given was pertinent to the inquiry of such committee or responsive to a question from such committee.

T.C.A. § 24-1-208. NEWS REPORTER'S PRIVILEGE

(a) A person engaged in gathering information for publication or broadcast connected with or employed by the news media or press, or who is independently engaged in gathering information for publication or broadcast, shall not be required by a court, a grand jury, the general assembly, or any administrative body, to disclose before the general assembly or any Tennessee court, grand jury, agency, department, or commission any information or the source of any information procured for publication or broadcast.

(b) Subsection (a) shall not apply with respect to the source of any allegedly defamatory information in any case where the defendant in a civil action for defamation asserts a defense based on the source of such information.

(c)(1) Any person seeking information or the source thereof protected under this section may apply for an order divesting such protection. Such application shall be made to the judge of the court having jurisdiction over the hearing, action, or other proceeding in which the information sought is pending.

(2) The application shall be granted only if the court after hearing the parties determines that the person seeking the information has shown by clear and convincing evidence that:

(A) There is probable cause to believe that the person from whom the information is sought has information which is clearly relevant to a specific probable violation of law;

(B) The person has demonstrated that the information sought cannot reasonably be obtained by alternative means; and

(C) The person has demonstrated a compelling and overriding public interest of the people of the State of Tennessee in the information.

(3)(A) Any order of the trial court may be appealed to the court of appeals in the same manner as other civil cases. The court of appeals shall make an independent determination of the applicability of the standards in this subsection to the facts in the record and shall not accord a presumption of correctness to the trial court's findings.

(B) The execution of or any proceeding to enforce a judgment divesting the protection of this section shall be stayed pending appeal upon the timely filing of a notice of appeal in accordance with Rule 3 of the Tennessee Rules of Civil Procedure, and the appeal shall be expedited upon the docket of the court of appeals upon the application of either party.

(C) Any order of the court of appeals may be appealed to the supreme court of Tennessee as provided by law.

T.C.A. §63-22-114. PROFESSIONAL COUNSELOR/MARITAL AND FAMILY THERAPIST/CLINICAL PASTORAL THERAPIST–CLIENT PRIVILEGE

The confidential relations and communications between licensed marital and family therapists, licensed professional counselors or certified clinical pastoral therapists and clients are placed upon the same basis as those provided by law between attorney and client, and nothing in this part shall be construed to require any such privileged communication to be disclosed. However, nothing contained within this section shall be construed to prevent disclosures of confidential communications in proceedings arising under title 37, chapter 1, part 4 concerning mandatory child abuse reports.

T.C.A. § 24-1-207. PSYCHIATRIST-PATIENT PRIVILEGE

(a) Communications between a patient and a licensed physician when practicing as a psychiatrist in the course of and in connection with a therapeutic counseling relationship regardless of whether the therapy is individual, joint, or group, are privileged in proceedings before judicial and quasi-judicial tribunals. Neither the psychiatrist nor any member of the staff may testify or be compelled to testify as to such communications or otherwise reveal them in such proceedings without consent of the patient except:

(1) In proceedings in which the patient raises the issue of the patient's mental or emotional condition;

(2) In proceedings for which the psychiatrist was ordered by the tribunal to examine the patient if the patient was advised that communications to the psychiatrist would not be privileged, but testimony as to the communications is admissible only on issues involving the patient's mental or emotional condition; and

(3) In proceedings to involuntarily hospitalize the patient under § 33-6-103 or § 33-6-104, if the psychiatrist decides that the patient is in need of care and treatment in a residential facility. Unless otherwise ordered by the court, the exception is limited to disclosures necessary to establish that the patient poses a substantial likelihood of serious harm requiring involuntary hospitalization under § 33-6-103 or § 33-6-104.

(b) When personally identifiable patient information is to be disclosed in a judicial or quasi-judicial proceeding or any other public proceeding, the authority conducting the proceeding shall take reasonable steps to prevent unnecessary exposure of such information to the public and to further this section's policy of protecting the right of privacy. Such steps may include screening of questions in pre-hearing conferences and in camera inspection of papers.

(c)(1) Privileged communications between a patient and a licensed physician when practicing as a psychiatrist in the course of and in connection with a therapeutic counseling relationship, regardless of whether the therapy is individual, joint, or group, may be disclosed without consent of the patient if:

(A) Such patient has made an actual threat to physically harm an identifiable victim or victims; and

(B) The treating psychiatrist makes a clinical judgment that the patient has the apparent capability to commit such an act and that it is more likely than not that in the near future the patient will carry out the threat.

(2) The psychiatrist may disclose patient communications to the extent necessary to warn or protect any potential victim. No civil or criminal action shall be instituted, nor shall liability be imposed due to the disclosure of otherwise confidential communications by a psychiatrist pursuant to this subsection.

T.C.A. § 63-11-213. PSYCHOLOGIST/PSYCHOLOGICAL EXAMINER-CLIENT PRIVILEGE

For the purposes of this chapter, the confidential relations and communications between licensed psychologist or psychological examiner and client are placed upon the same basis as those provided by law between attorney and client, and nothing in this chapter shall be construed to require any such privileged communication to be disclosed.

T.C.A. § 63-23-107. SOCIAL WORKER-CLIENT PRIVILEGE

(a) The confidential relations and communications between a client and a certified master social worker, or an independent practitioner of social work holding a valid certificate of registration, as defined in this chapter, are placed upon the same basis as those provided by law between licensed psychologists and psychological examiners and client, and nothing in this chapter shall be construed to require any such privileged communication to be disclosed.

(b) Nothing contained within this section shall be construed to prevent disclosure of confidential communications in proceedings arising under title 37, chapter 1, part 4 concerning mandatory child abuse reports.

T.C.A. § 24-1-201. SPOUSAL PRIVILEGE

(a) In either a civil or criminal proceeding, no married person has privilege to refuse to take the witness stand solely because that person's spouse is a party to the proceeding.

(b) In a civil proceeding, confidential communications between married persons are privileged and inadmissible if either spouse objects. This communications privilege shall not apply to proceedings between spouses or to proceedings concerning abuse of one (1) of the spouses or abuse of a minor in the custody of or under the dominion and control of either spouse, including, but not limited to, proceedings arising under title 36, chapter 1, part 1; title 37, chapter 1, parts 1, 4 and 6; title 37, chapter 2, part 4; and title 71, chapter 6, part 1. This confidential communications privilege shall not apply to any insured's obligations under a contract of insurance in civil proceedings.

(c) (1) In a criminal proceeding a marital confidential communication shall be privileged if:

(A) The communications originated in a confidence that they will not be disclosed;

(B) The element of confidentiality is essential to the full and satisfactory maintenance of the relation between the parties;

(C) The relation must be one which, in the opinion of the community, ought to be sedulously fostered; and

(D) The injury to the relation by disclosure of the communications outweighs the benefit gained for the correct disposal of litigation.

(2) Upon a finding that a marital communication is privileged, it shall be inadmissible if either spouse objects. Such communication privileges shall not apply to proceedings concerning abuse of one (1) of the spouses or abuse of a minor in the custody of or under the dominion and control of either spouse, including, but not limited to proceedings arising under title 37, chapter 1, parts 1 and 4; title 37, chapter 2, part 4; and title 71, chapter 6, part 1.

Advisory Commission Comments [2003].

Tenn. Code Ann. § 33-3-114. EXCEPTIONS TO EVIDENTIARY PRIVILEGE OF MENTAL HEALTH PROFESSIONALS

Notwithstanding any evidentiary privilege a qualified mental health professional may have, including §§ 24-1-207, 63-11-213, 63-22-114, and 63-23-107, the qualified mental health professional may be compelled to testify in:

(1) Judicial proceedings under this title to commit a person with mental illness, serious emotional disturbance, or developmental disability to treatment if the qualified mental health professional decides that the service recipient is in need of compulsory care and treatment;

(2) In proceedings for which the qualified mental health professional was ordered by the court to examine the service recipient if the service recipient was advised that communications to the qualified mental health professional would not be privileged.

Advisory Commission Comments [2010].

Delete from the 1999 comment the reference to Tenn. R. Crim. P. 6(k), which is not really a privilege.

Advisory Commission Comments [2012].

The Advisory Commission Comment [1999] was amended by deleting a reference to Tenn. Code Ann. § 63-6-219(e), which was repealed by Chapter 67, Tennessee Public Acts of 2011. In addition to repealing Tenn. Code Ann. § 63-6-219, Chapter 67 enacted the following privilege (using identical language in two separate statutes):

Tenn. Code Ann. §§ 63-1-150(d)(1) and 68-11-272(c)(1). QUALITY IMPROVEMENT COMMITTEE PRIVILEGE

Records of a QIC [Quality Improvement Committee] and testimony or statements by a healthcare organization's officers or directors, trustees, healthcare providers, administrative staff, employees or other committee members or attendees relating to activities of the QIC shall be confidential and privileged and shall be protected from direct or indirect means of discovery, subpoena or admission into evidence in any judicial or administrative proceeding. Any person who supplies information, testifies or makes statements as part of a QIC may not be required to provide information as to the information, testimony or statements provided to or made before such a committee or opinions formed by such person as a result of committee participation.

But see Tenn. Code Ann. § 63-1-150(a) (listing statutes to which Section 63-1-150 does not apply).

Inadvertent disclosure of privileged information or work product does not operate as a waiver if:
(1) the disclosure is inadvertent,
(2) the holder of the privilege or work-product protection took reasonable steps to prevent disclosure, and
(3) the holder promptly took reasonable steps to rectify the error.
[As added by order filed December 14, 2009, effective July 1, 2010;and by order filed January 8, 2018, effective July 1, 2018.]
Advisory Commission Comments [2010].
This language is taken from Federal Rule of Evidence 502(b). Compare Tennessee Rule of Civil Procedure 26.02(5) on discovery of electronically stored information.
Advisory Commission Comments [2018].
The 2018 amendment corrects a typographical error in the original text of the rule by adding the word "if" at the end of the introductory clause.

RULE 601: GENERAL RULE OF COMPETENCY.

Every person is presumed competent to be a witness except as otherwise provided in these rules or by statute.
[As amended by order entered January 24, 1992, effective July 1, 1992.]

Advisory Commission Comments.
This language is similar to T.C.A. § 24-1-101 [repealed], first sentence.
Virtually all witnesses may be permitted to testify: children, mentally incompetent persons, convicted felons. Rules 602 and 603 should be read in connection with this rule, however, because any witness must swear or affirm to tell the truth and must have personal knowledge of that truth. The common law rebuttably presumed children under fourteen incompetent, *Ball v. State*, 188 Tenn. 255, 219 S.W.2d 166 (1949), but the proposed rule is contra. See also T.C.A. § 24-1-101 [repealed], second sentence, making children under age thirteen competent in sexual offense prosecutions.
The most important statute referenced by the rule is the Dead Man Statute, T.C.A. § 24-1-203. It applies generally to prevent parties from testifying to transactions with a deceased person in actions by or against estates. While the statute occasionally causes proof problems, the rule leaves it intact. See also T.C.A. § 24-1-202 [repealed] on incompetents' estates.

Advisory Commission Comments [1992].
The amendment removes the earlier language requiring "of sufficient capacity to understand the obligation of an oath or affirmation"and establishes a rebuttable presumption of competency. Note, however, that Rule 602 requires lay witnesses to have personal knowledge of matters, and Rule 603 requires all witnesses to swear or affirm they will tell the truth.

RULE 602: LACK OF PERSONAL KNOWLEDGE.

A witness may not testify to a matter unless evidence is introduced sufficient to support a finding that the witness has personal knowledge of the matter. Evidence to prove personal knowledge may, but need not, consist of the witness's own testimony. This rule is subject to the provisions of Rule 703 relating to opinion testimony by expert witnesses.

Advisory Commission Comments.
Basic to relevancy concepts is that a witness must know about the subject matter of testimony. This is the familiar requirement of first-hand knowledge.
Under Rule 703, experts may base an opinion on the factual findings of others. Also, party admissions need not be based on first-hand knowledge.

RULE 603: OATH OR AFFIRMATION.

Before testifying, every witness shall be required to declare that the witness will testify truthfully by oath or affirmation, administered in a form calculated to awaken the witness's conscience and impress the witness's mind with the duty to do so.

<u>Advisory Commission Comments.</u>
Witnesses have already been required to take an oath or affirmation. T.C.A. § 24-1-101 [repealed], third sentence, is similar to the rule.

RULE 604: INTERPRETERS.

An interpreter is subject to the provisions of these rules and applicable statutes relating to qualifications as an expert and the administration of an oath or affirmation to make a true interpretation.
[Amended by order filed December 29, 2005, effective July 1, 2006.]

<u>Advisory Commission Comments.</u>
Interpreters must fulfill two requirements: expertise in translating and willingness to swear or affirm. T.C.A. § 24-1-211 details the qualifications of sign language interpreters.

<u>Advisory Commission Comment [2006].</u>
The last word is changed from "translation" to "interpretation."

RULE 605: COMPETENCY OF JUDGE AS WITNESS.

The judge or chancellor presiding at the trial may not testify in that trial. No objection need be made in order to preserve the point.

<u>Advisory Commission Comments.</u>

The rule would change Tennessee law. T.C.A. § 24-1-205 [repealed] permits trial testimony by a presiding judge. The commission thought it wiser to avoid this awkward practice. See also Canon 3 of the Code of Judicial Conduct.
Of course a judge could testify in a later collateral attack proceeding. The subsequent proceeding would not be "that trial."
The rule does not change a judge's power to notice facts or law under Rules 201 and 202.

RULE 606: COMPETENCY OF JUROR AS WITNESS.

(a) At the Trial. A member of the jury may not testify as a witness before that jury in the trial of the case in which the juror is sitting. No objection need be made in order to preserve the point.
(b) Inquiry into Validity of Verdict or Indictment. Upon an inquiry into the validity of a verdict or indictment, a juror may not testify as to any matter or statement occurring during the course of the jury's deliberations or to the effect of anything upon any juror's mind or emotions as influencing that juror to assent to or dissent from the verdict or indictment or concerning the juror's mental processes, except that a juror may testify on the question of whether extraneous prejudicial information was improperly brought to the jury's attention, whether any outside influence was improperly brought to bear upon any juror, or whether the jurors agreed in advance to be bound by a quotient or gambling verdict without further discussion; nor may a juror's affidavit or evidence of any statement by the juror concerning a matter about which the juror would be precluded from testifying be received for these purposes.
[As amended by order filed January 23, 2001, effective July 1, 2001.]

<u>Advisory Commission Comments.</u>
While there is no Tennessee precedent, jurors could and did testify at early common law. This proposed rule would prevent a juror from switching from jury box to witness stand during the course of a trial.
After verdict, part (b) would come into play. A juror may testify or submit an affidavit in connection with a motion for new trial, but only in the limited circumstances of:
(1) "Extraneous prejudicial information" finding its way into the jury room,
(2) Improper outside pressure on a juror, or
(3) A quotient or gambling verdict.
This rule is the same as that adopted in *State v. Blackwell*, 664 S.W.2d 686 (Tenn. 1984).

RULE 607: WHO MAY IMPEACH?

The credibility of a witness may be attacked by any party, including the party calling the witness.

<u>Advisory Commission Comments.</u>

The rule would abolish Tennessee's common law prohibition against impeaching one's own witness —the voucher rule. The present rule finds expression in King v. State, 187 Tenn. 431, 215 S.W.2d 813 (1948); *Record v. Chickasaw Cooperage Co.*, 108 Tenn. 657, 69 S.W. 334 (1902).

The Commission believed that requiring a lawyer calling a witness to vouch for the witness's credibility too often unfairly restricts proof. Obviously there is no choice over who witnesses facts. In some instances, rigid enforcement of the voucher rule has caused Constitutional error. See *Chambers v. Mississippi*, 410 U.S. 284, 93 S. Ct. 1038, 35 L. Ed. 2d 297 (1973).
  See Rule 611 for the mode and order of interrogation.

<u>Advisory Commission Comments [2000].</u>

Decisional law prohibits a lawyer from calling a witness —knowing the testimony will be adverse to the lawyer's position —solely to impeach that witness by an inconsistent statement. See the June 1999 issue of the Tennessee Bar Journal at page 23 and Cohen et alia, Tennessee Law of Evidence (3d ed.) at § 613.1.

RULE 608: EVIDENCE OF CHARACTER AND CONDUCT OF WITNESS.

(a) Opinion and Reputation Evidence of Character - The credibility of a witness may be attacked or supported by evidence in the form of opinion or reputation, but subject to these limitations: (1) the evidence may refer only to character for truthfulness or untruthfulness, and (2) the evidence of truthful character is admissible only after the character of the witness for truthfulness has been attacked.
(b) Specific Instances of Conduct - Specific instances of conduct of a witness for the purpose of attacking or supporting the witness's character for truthfulness, other than convictions of crime as provided in Rule 609, may not be proved by extrinsic evidence. They may, however, if probative of truthfulness or untruthfulness and under the following conditions, be inquired into on cross-examination of the witness concerning the witness's character for truthfulness or untruthfulness or concerning the character for truthfulness or untruthfulness of another witness as to which the character witness being cross-examined has testified. The conditions which must be satisfied

before allowing inquiry on cross-examination about such conduct probative solely of truthfulness or untruthfulness are:

(1) The court upon request must hold a hearing outside the jury's presence and must determine that the alleged conduct has probative value and that a reasonable factual basis exists for the inquiry;

(2) The conduct must have occurred no more than ten years before commencement of the action or prosecution, but evidence of a specific instance of conduct not qualifying under this paragraph (2) is admissible if the proponent gives to the adverse party sufficient advance notice of intent to use such evidence to provide the adverse party with a fair opportunity to contest the use of such evidence and the court determines in the interests of justice that the probative value of that evidence, supported by specific facts and circumstances, substantially outweighs its prejudicial effect; and

 (3) If the witness to be impeached is the accused in a criminal prosecution, the State must give the accused reasonable written notice of the impeaching conduct before trial, and the court upon request must determine that the conduct's probative value on credibility outweighs its unfair prejudicial effect on the substantive issues. The court may rule on the admissibility of such proof prior to the trial but in any event shall rule prior to the testimony of the accused. If the court makes a final determination that such proof is admissible for impeachment purposes, the accused need not actually testify at the trial to later challenge the propriety of the determination.

The giving of testimony, whether by an accused or by any other witness, does not operate as a waiver of the witness's privilege against self-incrimination when examined with respect to matters which relate only to character for truthfulness.

(c) Juvenile Conduct - Evidence of specific instances of conduct of a witness committed while the witness was a juvenile is generally not admissible under this rule. The court may, however, allow evidence of such conduct of a witness other than the accused in a criminal case if the conduct would be admissible to attack the credibility of an adult and the court is satisfied that admission in evidence is necessary for a fair determination in a civil action or criminal proceeding.

[As amended by order entered January 25, 1991, effective July 1, 199, and by order filed January 6, 2005, effective July 1, 2005.]

Advisory Commission Comments.

Part (a) admits opinion as well as community reputation to prove character. Presently Tennessee restricts proof to reputation evidence. *Ford v. Ford*, 26 Tenn. 91, 100-01 (1846). The proposed change is minimal, however, because Tennessee has allowed a character witness on the credibility issue to opine that the fact witness should or should not be believed. *Ford v. Ford*, 26 Tenn. 92, 102 (1846).

Part (b) reflects the Supreme Court's view of impeachment by prior bad acts. *State v. Morgan*, 541 S.W.2d 385 (Tenn. 1976), incorporated F.R.Evid. 608(b) into Tennessee case law. The proposed rule is even more specific than the federal version. It requires a jury-out hearing on probative value and basis for cross-examination, relatively recent misconduct, and notice plus analytical weighing of probative value versus unfair prejudice.

To the extent that *State v. Caruthers*, 676 S.W.2d 936 (Tenn. 1984), can be construed as allowing cross-examination about a prior act of rape to impeach, the proposal would change that result.

If the witness makes a sweeping claim of good conduct on direct examination, that claim may open the door to cross-examination without pretrial notice and with a lower standard of probativeness, as rebuttal of the broad claim would itself tend to show untruthfulness. Also, there may be instances where the prosecution would not discover the accused's bad acts until after the trial begins, making pretrial notice impossible; in such cases immediate notice and a hearing on the issue before the accused testifies should satisfy the spirit of the rule.

Note that the accused's failure to take the stand in face of an adverse ruling on admissibility of a prior bad act does not waive the right to assign error on appeal.

Part (c) conforms juvenile bad acts admissibility to the principles used with juvenile adjudications. See Rule 609(d).

Advisory Commission Comments [1991].
This is a technical amendment.

Advisory Commission Comments [2005].
Substituting "character for truthfulness" in place of "credibility" at the beginning and end of Rule 608(b) clarifies that contradiction impeachment by extrinsic evidence is permissible.

RULE 609: IMPEACHMENT BY EVIDENCE OF CONVICTION OF CRIME.

(a) General Rule - For the purpose of attacking the credibility of a witness, evidence that the witness has been convicted of a crime may be admitted if the following procedures and conditions are satisfied:

(1) The witness must be asked about the conviction on cross-examination. If the witness denies having been convicted, the conviction may be established by public record. If the witness denies being the person named in the public record, identity may be established by other evidence.

(2) The crime must be punishable by death or imprisonment in excess of one year under the law under which the witness was convicted or, if not so punishable, the crime must have involved dishonesty or false statement.

(3) If the witness to be impeached is the accused in a criminal prosecution, the State must give the accused reasonable written notice of the impeaching conviction before trial, and the court upon request must determine that the conviction's probative value on credibility outweighs its unfair prejudicial effect on the substantive issues. The court may rule on the admissibility of such proof prior to the trial but in any event shall rule prior to the testimony of the accused. If the court makes a final determination that such proof is admissible for impeachment purposes, the accused need not actually testify at the trial to later challenge the propriety of the determination.

(b) Time Limit - Evidence of a conviction under this rule is not admissible if a period of more than ten years has elapsed between the date of release from confinement and commencement of the action or prosecution; if the witness was not confined, the ten-year period is measured from the date of conviction rather than release. Evidence of a conviction not qualifying under the preceding sentence is admissible if the proponent gives to the adverse party sufficient advance notice of intent to use such evidence to provide the adverse party with a fair opportunity to contest the use of such evidence and the court determines in the interests of justice that the probative value of the conviction, supported by specific facts and circumstances, substantially outweighs its prejudicial effect.

(c) Effect of Pardon - Evidence of a conviction is not admissible under this rule if (1) the conviction has been the subject of a pardon based on a finding of the rehabilitation of the person convicted and that person has not been convicted of a subsequent crime which was punishable by death or imprisonment in excess of one year, or (2) the conviction has been the subject of a pardon based on a finding of innocence.

(d) Juvenile Adjudications - Evidence of juvenile adjudications is generally not admissible under this rule. The court may, however, allow evidence of a juvenile adjudication of a witness other than the accused in a criminal case if conviction of the offense would be admissible to attack the credibility of an adult and the court is satisfied that admission in evidence is necessary for a fair determination in a civil action or criminal proceeding.

(e) Pendency of Appeal - The pendency of an appeal of a conviction does not render evidence of that conviction inadmissible. Evidence of the pendency of an appeal is admissible.
<u>Advisory Commission Comments.</u>

The Supreme Court adopted F.R.Evid. 609(a) & (b) in *State v. Morgan*, 541 S.W.2d 385 (Tenn. 1976), and thereby rejected the old "moral turpitude" criterion for admissibility of convictions to impeach. Proposed Tennessee Rule 609(a) takes Morgan at face value and lists its essential elements:

(1) The time of proof ordinarily is during cross-examination, but the witness's denial triggers extrinsic evidence. This rule does not preclude questions about prior convictions during direct examination.

(2) Only felony convictions or those misdemeanor convictions involving dishonesty are competent for impeachment. See *State v. Butler*, 626 S.W.2d 6 (Tenn. 1981), for the Supreme Court's view that theft crimes involve dishonesty. The rule is consistent with Butler.

(3) When the witness in a criminal trial is the accused, the prosecution "must"give pretrial notice and the trial judge "must"make a determination before the accused elects to testify or not that the probative value of the conviction "on credibility"is greater than its "unfair prejudicial effect on the substantive issues."To the extent that *State v. Sheffield*, 676 S.W.2d 542 (Tenn. 1984), is inconsistent, the proposal would change the result.

Note that the accused who does not take the witness stand because of an unfavorable ruling on admissibility of a prior conviction can nonetheless raise error on appeal.

For witnesses not covered by 609(a)(3), the balancing test is different. Rule 403 applies, and a conviction would be admissible to impeach unless "its probative value is substantially outweighed by the danger of unfair prejudice"or other criteria listed in that rule.

Part (b) of proposed Rule 609 restates and hopefully clarifies Morgan language concerning inadmissibility of stale convictions. To avoid the mistaken exclusion of convictions "ten years old," the rule separates convictions with time served from those where the convict served no prison time. Normally, ten years would be measured from release from jail to commencement of prosecution.

Even old convictions can be used in certain instances, but the proposed rule requires a weighing ("substantially outweighs") of probative value versus undue prejudicial effect, with a specific factual determination by the trial judge.
Part (c) excludes only those convictions of witnesses pardoned because of rehabilitation or innocence.

Part (d) follows the current philosophy expressed in T.C.A. § 37-1-133(b) and *State v. Butler,* 626 S.W.2d 6 (Tenn. 1981). Constitutional confrontation issues may require admitting the juvenile record of a witness testifying against the criminal accused. See *Davis v. Alaska,* 415 U.S. 308 (1974).

Part (e) permits impeachment by a conviction undergoing appeal because, under Tennessee law, the convict is presumed guilty after judgment.

Advisory Commission Comments [2001].

The Tennessee Supreme Court suggested in *State v. Galmore,* 994 S.W.2d 120 (1999), and *State v. Taylor,* 993 S.W.2d 33 (1999), that the accused in a criminal trial may need to make a jury-out offer of proof in order to reverse the trial court for an erroneous ruling that a conviction is admissible to impeach. Such error might otherwise be harmless.

RULE 610: RELIGIOUS BELIEFS OR OPINIONS.

Evidence of the beliefs or opinions of a witness on matters of religion is not admissible for the purpose of showing that by reason of their nature the witness's credibility is impaired or enhanced.

Advisory Commission Comments.
The rule prohibits any use of religious beliefs either to impeach or enhance a witness's credibility. Adoption of the rule would bring a salutary change to Tennessee law in the Commission's view. Cf. T.C.A. § 24-1-102 [repealed].

RULE 611: MODE AND ORDER OF INTERROGATION AND PRESENTATION.

(a) Control by Court - The court shall exercise appropriate control over the presentation of evidence and conduct of the trial when necessary to avoid abuse by counsel.

(b) Scope of Cross-Examination - A witness may be cross-examined on any matter relevant to any issue in the case, including credibility, except as provided in paragraph (c)(2) of this rule.

(c) Leading Questions -
(1) Leading questions should not be used on the direct examination of a witness except as may be necessary to develop the witness's testimony. Leading questions should be permitted on cross-examination.

(2) When a party calls a hostile witness, an adverse party (or an officer, director, or managing agent of a public or private corporation or of a partnership, association, or individual proprietorship which is an adverse party), or a witness identified with an adverse party, interrogation may be by leading questions. The scope of cross-examination under this paragraph shall be limited to the subject matter of direct examination, and cross-examination may be by leading questions.
[As amended by order filed December 21, 2010, effective July 1, 2011.]

Advisory Commission Comments.
Part (a) recognizes the inherent power of a court to control trial conduct to prevent lawyers from abusing the process.

Part (b) retains the English rule permitting wide-open scope of cross-examination historically favored in Tennessee. *Sands v. Southern Railway Co.,* 108 Tenn. 1, 64 S.W. 478 (1901), is the leading case.
Part (c) attempts to resolve leading question problems. Generally a lawyer may lead on cross but not on direct.

Advisory Commission Comments [2011].
Amended Rule 611 allows a lawyer to ask leading questions when calling a "witness identified with an adverse party" in all civil and criminal proceedings.

Advisory Commission Comments [2017].
Nothing in these rules prohibits the court in its inherent authority from permitting a suitable animal, toy, or support person to accompany a witness who is shown to be at risk for being unable to communicate effectively without the aid of such comfort. See *State v. Juan Jose Reyes*, No. M2015-00504-CCA-R3-CD, 2016 WL 3090904 (Tenn. Crim. App. May 24, 2016), *perm. app. denied* (Tenn. Sept. 23, 2016).

RULE 612: WRITING USED TO REFRESH MEMORY.

If a witness uses a writing while testifying to refresh memory for the purpose of testifying, an adverse party is entitled to inspect it, to cross-examine the witness thereon, and to introduce in evidence those portions which relate to the testimony of the witness. If it is claimed that the writing contains matters not related to the subject matter of the testimony, the court shall examine the writing in camera, excise any portions not so related, and order delivery of the remainder to the party entitled thereto. Any portion withheld over objections shall be preserved and made available to the appellate court in the event of appeal. If a writing is not produced or delivered pursuant to order under this rule, the court shall make any order justice requires; in criminal cases when the prosecution elects not to comply, the order shall be one striking the testimony or, if the court in its discretion determines that the interests of justice so require, declaring a mistrial.

Advisory Commission Comments.
Tennessee trial lawyers have long used this procedure for refreshing a witness's recollection, and this rule simply reflects traditional law. Only writings used "while testifying" are subject to opposing counsel's inspection. See also T.R.Crim.P. 26.2.

Only if a witness's memory requires refreshing should a writing be used by the witness. The direct examiner should lay a foundation for necessity, show the witness the writing, take back the writing, and ask the witness to testify from refreshed memory.

(a) Examining Witness Concerning Prior Statement - In examining a witness concerning a prior statement made by the witness, whether written or not, the statement need not be shown nor its contents disclosed to the witness at that time, but on request the same shall be shown or disclosed to opposing counsel.

(b) Extrinsic Evidence of Prior Inconsistent Statement of Witness - Extrinsic evidence of a prior inconsistent statement by a witness is not admissible unless and until the witness is afforded an opportunity to explain or deny the same and the opposite party is afforded an opportunity to interrogate the witness thereon, or the interests of justice otherwise require. This provision does not apply to admissions of a party-opponent as defined in Rule 803(1.2).

(c) Opinions - A prior statement in opinion form is admissible to impeach testimony.

[Amended by order filed January 31, 2003, effective July 1, 2003.]

Advisory Commission Comments.

The rule eliminates any necessity of showing an inconsistent writing to a fact witness under impeachment attack. The only requirement is that, where the impeaching lawyer introduces extrinsic evidence of the inconsistent statement, the fact witness must be "afforded an opportunity to explain or deny." The rule will not change drastically Tennessee procedure. Compare *Moore v. Bettis,* 30 Tenn. 67 (1850), with *Titus v. State*, 66 Tenn. 132 (1874).

Part (c) would change such hypertechnical results as that reached in *Saunders v. City & Suburban Railroad*, 99 Tenn. 130, 41 S.W. 1031 (1897), excluding a prior inconsistent statement characterized as an "opinion". Obviously an opinion inconsistent with a fact should be admissible.

Advisory Commission Comment [2003].

Paragraph (b) is amended to add the words "and until." The effect is to incorporate the holding in *State v. Martin*, 964 S.W.2d 564 (Tenn. 1998): "extrinsic evidence remains inadmissible until the witness either denies or equivocates as to having made the prior inconsistent statement."

Note that Rule 806 does not require a foundation before impeaching a hearsay declarant by inconsistent statement.

(a) Calling by court - The court may not call witnesses except in extraordinary circumstances or except as provided for court-appointed experts in Rule 706, and all parties are entitled to cross-examine witnesses thus called.

(b) Interrogation by Court - The court may interrogate witnesses.

(c) Objections - Objections to the calling of witnesses by the court or to interrogation by it may be made at the time or at the next available opportunity when the jury is not present.

Advisory Commission Comments.

Ordinarily the trial judge may question but not call lay witnesses. Rule 706 details procedures for calling court-appointed expert witnesses in a bench trial.

In questioning a witness, the judge must avoid "commenting on the evidence"in violation of the Tennessee Constitution, Art. VI, Sec. 9.

RULE 615: EXCLUSION OF WITNESSES.

At the request of a party the court shall order witnesses, including rebuttal witnesses, excluded at trial or other adjudicatory hearing. In the court's discretion, the requested sequestration may be effective before voir dire, but in any event shall be effective before opening statements. The court shall order all persons not to disclose by any means to excluded witnesses any live trial testimony or exhibits created in the courtroom by a witness. This rule does not authorize exclusion of (1) a party who is a natural person, or (2) a person designated by counsel for a party that is not a natural person, or (3) a person whose presence is shown by a party to be essential to the presentation of the party's cause. This rule does not forbid testimony of a witness called at the rebuttal stage of a hearing if, in the court's discretion, counsel is genuinely surprised and demonstrates a need for rebuttal testimony from an unsequestered witness.
[Amended by order effective July 1, 1997.]

Advisory Commission Comments.
The Commission took a realistic view of the sequestration rule. If "The Rule"is to be meaningful, witnesses should not only be instructed to refrain from discussing their courtroom testimony, but lawyers and others should be instructed not to transmit what witnesses say in court. Note that rebuttal witnesses are covered by the proposal, contrary to current Tennessee practice.
This rule does not prohibit a witness from reviewing depositions of other witnesses before testifying.

Under subsection (3) in the final sentence, the court has discretion to allow a witness to remain in the courtroom or even at counsel table if the witness's presence is "essential to the presentation of the party's cause." Such a witness might be an expert witness a lawyer needs to help the lawyer understand opposing testimony. Also, an expert witness who is to learn facts only through hearing testimony in court could be allowed to sit in the courtroom under this subsection. See Rule 703.

If a witness inadvertently and unintentionally hears some trial testimony, the sense of the rule would permit the judge to allow the witness to testify if fair under the circumstances.

Advisory Commission Comments [1992].
Under Rule 101, the Evidence Rules apply to rulings in "trial courts." Strictly speaking, Rule 615 is intended to apply only to sequestration of witnesses at trial. A lawyer who wishes to exclude nonparties from oral depositions must resort to T.R.Civ.P. 26.03(5), allowing on motion a protective order" that discovery be conducted with no one present except persons designated by the court."

<u>**Advisory Commission Comments [1997].**</u>
The amended rule contains three changes. One gives the court discretion to delay sequestration until after voir dire, perhaps because of a need to ask prospective jurors whether they know the witnesses.

The second change modifies the second category of persons not sequested. A "party that is not a natural person" includes, among other entities, a corporation and the State of Tennessee. Consequently, the prosecuting attorney could designate a crime victim, a relative of a crime victim, or an investigating officer. Like category (1), category (2) is a matter of right. Category (3), in contrast, is a matter of judicial discretion.

The third change is addition of a sentence at the end of the rule to give the court authority to make an exception for rebuttal witnesses. Such an exception requires, however, a dual showing of genuine surprise and demonstrable need.

Note that the rule prohibits disclosure of live testimony "by any means." A lawyer may mention subject matter to a witness not yet called, even though the subject matter has been raised by evidence. Care must be taken, however, to avoid implying to the potential witness what an earlier witness said from the stand.

<u>**Advisory Commission Comment [2004].**</u>
Expert witnesses generally should be considered "essential persons" and therefore should not be sequestered. In *State v. Bane*, 57 S.W.3d 411, 423 (Tenn. 2001), the Court stated: "[W]e believe that the dangers Rule 615 is intended to prevent generally do not arise with regard to expert witnesses in any proceeding."

RULE 616: IMPEACHMENT BY BIAS OR PREJUDICE.

A party may offer evidence by cross-examination, extrinsic evidence, or both, that a witness is biased in favor of or prejudiced against a party or another witness.

<u>**Advisory Commission Comments.**</u>
Bias is an important ground for impeachment. See *Creeping Bear v. State*, 113 Tenn. 322, 87 S.W. 653 (1905).

RULE 617: IMPEACHMENT BY IMPAIRED CAPACITY.

A party may offer evidence that a witness suffered from impaired capacity at the time of an occurrence or testimony.

<u>**Advisory Commission Comments.**</u>
Only impaired capacity at "occurrence or testimony" will impeach.

RULE 618: IMPEACHMENT OF EXPERT BY LEARNED TREATISES.

To the extent called to the attention of an expert witness upon cross-examination or relied upon by the witness in direct examination, statements contained in published treatises, periodicals, or pamphlets on a subject of history, medicine, or other science or art, established as a reliable authority by the testimony or admission of the witness, by other expert testimony, or by judicial notice, may be used to impeach the expert witness's credibility but may not be received as substantive evidence.

Advisory Commission Comments.

The rule restates the current Tennessee view. *Sale v. Eichberg*, 105 Tenn. 333, 59 S.W. 1020 (1900); *McCay v. Mitchell*, 62 Tenn. App. 424, 463 S.W.2d 710 (1970).

Article VII. Opinions and Expert Testimony

RULE 701: OPINION TESTIMONY BY LAY WITNESSES.

(a) Generally - If a witness is not testifying as an expert, the witness's testimony in the form of opinions or inferences is limited to those opinions or inferences which are

(1) rationally based on the perception of the witness and

(2) helpful to a clear understanding of the witness's testimony or the determination of a fact in issue.

(b) Value - A witness may testify to the value of the witness's own property or services.

[Amended by order effective July 1, 1996.]

Advisory Commission Comments [1996].

This rule was amended because the former rule precluded any lay opinion if the lay witness could substitute facts for opinion.

RULE 702: TESTIMONY BY EXPERTS.

If scientific, technical, or other specialized knowledge will substantially assist the trier of fact to understand the evidence or to determine a fact in issue, a witness qualified as an expert by knowledge, skill, experience, training, or education may testify in the form of an opinion or otherwise.

Advisory Commission Comments [2001].

The Frye test no longer exists in Tennessee. In *McDaniel v. CSX Transportation, Inc.*, 955 S.W.2d 257 (1997), the Tennessee Supreme Court listed five nonexclusive factors taken from the federal case of *Daubert v. Merrell Dow Pharmaceuticals*, 509 U.S. 579 (1993):

"(1) whether scientific evidence has been tested and the methodology with which it has been tested;

"(2) whether the evidence has been subjected to peer review or publication;

"(3) whether a potential rate of error is known;

"(4) whether, as formerly required by Frye, the evidence is generally accepted in the scientific community; and

"(5) whether the expert's research in the field has been conducted independent of litigation."

RULE 703: BASES OF OPINION TESTIMONY BY EXPERTS.

The facts or data in the particular case upon which an expert bases an opinion or inference may be those perceived by or made known to the expert at or before the hearing. If of a type reasonably relied upon by experts in the particular field in forming opinions or inferences upon the subject, the facts or data need not be admissible in evidence. Facts or data that are otherwise inadmissible shall not be disclosed to the jury by the proponent of the opinion or inference unless the court determines that their probative value in assisting the jury to evaluate the expert's opinion substantially outweighs their prejudicial effect. The court shall disallow testimony in the form of an opinion or inference if the underlying facts or data indicate lack of trustworthiness.

[As amended by order filed January 8, 2009, effective July 1, 2009.]

Advisory Commission Comments.
Experts in the field may base opinions on facts not in evidence under this rule. Requisite foundations are that (1) the facts must be "reasonably relied upon by experts in the particular field" and (2) the facts must be trustworthy. With such foundations, inadmissible hearsay could support an admissible expert opinion.
New Jersey Zinc Co. v. Cole, 532 S.W.2d 246 (Tenn. 1975), allows a treating doctor to base an opinion on reports of other professionals.
If the bases of expert testimony are not independently admissible, the trial judge should either prohibit the jury from hearing the foundation testimony or should deliver a cautionary instruction. Unfairly prejudicial facts or data should be dealt with under Rule 403. With respect to cross-examination, see Rule 705.

Advisory Commission Comments [2009].
The third sentence is new. Normally a jury should not be allowed to hear the reliable but inadmissible bases underlying an expert's opinion.

RULE 704: OPINION ON ULTIMATE ISSUE.

Testimony in the form of an opinion or inference otherwise admissible is not objectionable because it embraces an ultimate issue to be decided by the trier of fact.

Advisory Commission Comments.
The Supreme Court has already approved this language. *City of Columbia v. C.F.W. Construction Co.,* 557 S.W.2d 734 (Tenn. 1977). But *Blackburn v. Murphy,* 737 S.W.2d 529 (Tenn. 1987), places limitations on lay witnesses testifying to some ultimate issues, such as whether an accident was unavoidable.

Advisory Commission Comments [1996].
One ultimate issue is outside the scope of expert testimony. T.C.A. § 39-11-501 provides that "no expert witness may testify as to whether the defendant was or was not insane."

RULE 705: DISCLOSURE OF FACTS OR DATA UNDERLYING EXPERT OPINION.

The expert may testify in terms of opinion or inference and give reasons without prior disclosure of the underlying facts or data, unless the court requires otherwise. The expert may in any event be required to disclose the underlying facts or data on cross-examination.

Advisory Commission Comments.
This rule gives a lawyer the option of not using a hypothetical question in examining an expert; the lawyer can ask the expert simply to state an opinion. Tennessee presently requires the hypothetical unless the expert bases testimony on personal observation. See, e.g., *Valentine v. Conchemco,* 588 S.W.2d 871 (Tenn. Ct. App. 1979).

(a) Appointment - The court may not appoint expert witnesses of its own selection on issues to be tried by a jury except as provided otherwise by law. As to bench-tried issues, the court may on its own motion or on the motion of any party enter an order to show cause why expert witnesses should not be appointed and may request the parties to submit nominations. The court ordinarily should appoint expert witnesses agreed upon by the parties, but in appropriate cases, for reasons stated on the record, the court may appoint expert witnesses of its own selection. An expert witness shall not be appointed by the court unless the witness consents to act. A witness so appointed shall be informed of the witness's duties by the court in writing, a copy of which shall be filed with the clerk, or at a conference in which the parties shall have opportunity to participate. A witness so appointed shall advise the parties of the witness's findings, the witness's deposition may be taken by any party, and the witness may be called to testify by the court or any party. The witness shall be subject to cross-examination by each party, including a party calling the witness.

(b) Compensation - Expert witnesses so appointed are entitled to reasonable compensation in whatever sum the court may allow. The compensation thus fixed is payable from funds which may be provided by law in criminal cases and civil actions and condemnation proceedings. In other civil actions and proceedings the compensation shall be paid by the parties in such proportion and at such time as the court directs and thereafter charged in like manner as other costs.

(c) Disclosure of Appointment - Where a court-appointed expert is permitted otherwise by law to testify on an issue to be tried by a jury, no one may disclose to the jury the fact that the court appointed the expert witness.

(d) Parties' Experts of Own Selection - Nothing in this rule limits the parties in calling expert witnesses of their own selection.

Advisory Commission Comments.

The Commission was wary of the undue impact a court-appointed expert might have on a jury, and the rule prohibits such experts in jury trials unless expressly permitted by statute. Even where the trial court wants its own expert in a bench trial, the judge normally should defer to the parties' suggestions. Either party may discover and cross-examine the court's expert.

RULE 801: DEFINITIONS.

The following definitions apply under this article:

(a) Statement - A "statement" is (1) an oral or written assertion or (2) nonverbal conduct of a person if it is intended by the person as an assertion.
(b) Declarant - A "declarant" is a person who makes a statement.

(c) Hearsay - "Hearsay" is a statement, other than one made by the declarant while testifying at the trial or hearing, offered in evidence to prove the truth of the matter asserted.

Advisory Commission Comments.
This rule, generally defining hearsay, is the first of a series covering hearsay evidence. The next provision, Rule 802, states the general rule that hearsay evidence is inadmissible unless otherwise provided by law. Rules 803 and 804 describe hearsay exceptions. Rule 805 deals with multiple hearsay, and Rule 806 provides a general rule for impeaching hearsay declarants.

Except for the definition of conduct as hearsay, Rule 801 restates Tennessee common law. Part (a) makes hearsay only such nonverbal conduct as the declarant actor intends as an assertion. The common law, stemming from *Wright v. Tatham*, 112 Eng. Rep. 488 (Exch. Ch. 1837), included in the hearsay definition assertions that might be inferred from the conduct but that were unintended by the actor. Consequently, Tennessee has defined flight from a crime scene as hearsay, although the courts admit the evidence through the exception for party admissions. Under the proposed rule, the evidence would be admissible as nonhearsay, the declarant obviously not intending to assert guilt by flight.

RULE 802: HEARSAY RULE.

Hearsay is not admissible except as provided by these rules or otherwise by law.

Advisory Commission Comments.
The rule does not change Tennessee law.

RULE 803: HEARSAY EXCEPTIONS.

The following are not excluded by the hearsay rule:

(1) [Reserved.]

Advisory Commission Comments.
The proposed rules contain no present sense impression exception.

(1.1) Prior Statement of Identification by Witness. A statement of identification of a person made after perceiving the person if the declarant testifies at the trial or hearing and is subject to cross-examination concerning the statement.

<u>**Advisory Commission Comments.**</u>
Tennessee recognizes declarations of eye-witness identification as an exception to hearsay exclusion, and the rule generally follows Tennessee precedent. Note that the declarant must also be a witness, affording at least delayed cross-examination as to the extrajudicial statement. Note also, however, that witnesses other than the declarant may testify about the identifying declaration. Perhaps the rule changes Tennessee law in this respect. See *Blankenship v. State*, 432 S.W.2d 679, 684 (Tenn. Crim. App. 1967).

(1.2) Admission by Party-Opponent. A statement offered against a party that is (A) the party's own statement in either an individual or a representative capacity, or (B) a statement in which the party has manifested an adoption or belief in its truth, or (C) a statement by a person authorized by the party to make a statement concerning the subject, or (D) a statement by an agent or servant concerning a matter within the scope of the agency or employment made during the existence of the relationship under circumstances qualifying the statement as one against the declarant's interest regardless of declarant's availability, or (E) a statement by a co-conspirator of a party during the course of and in furtherance of the conspiracy, or (F) a statement by a person in privity of estate with the party. An admission is not excluded merely because the statement is in the form of an opinion. Statements admissible under this exception are not conclusive.

<u>**Advisory Commission Comments.**</u>
Most of the rule embodies Tennessee common law. In part (D), though, present law is extended to clearly allow an agent's post-accident declarations to come in against the principal if the subject matter of the declarations is "within the scope of the agency." A driver who tells bystanders about driving mistakes may face those declarations in court, and likewise the driver's employer may have to deal with these vicarious admissions at trial. In the absence of a rule such as that proposed, Tennessee has excluded such declarations. *Citizens' Street R.R. Co. v. Howard*, 102 Tenn. 474, 52 S.W. 864 (1899).
Other requirements for vicarious admissions are (1) that the agency relationship exist at the time of a declaration and (2) that the declarant's statement be against his or her own interest. The latter proviso is to prevent agents and employees from gratuitously harming superiors for their own benefit.
The rule at part (F) retains common law admissibility of declarations by predecessors in title.
The final sentence is intended to abolish the distinction between evidentiary (unsworn) and judicial (sworn) admissions. Unless made conclusive by statute or another court rule, such as Tenn. R. Civ. P. 36.02 on requests for admission, party admissions are subject to being explained away by contradictory proof. But the final sentence is not intended to affect the doctrine of judicial estoppel. That doctrine involves two separate lawsuits and bars contradiction by a party in the second suit of that party's sworn statement in the first suit. See *Marcus v. Marcus*, 993 S.W.2d 596 (Tenn. 1999). In contrast the last sentence of this evidence rule contemplates a single lawsuit in which a party's admissions, sworn or not, can be contradicted.
This rule changes the law as stated in Tennessee decisions excluding party admissions phrased in terms of fault. See, e.g., *King v. Leeman*, 30 Tenn. App. 206, 204 S.W.2d 384 (1946), excluding

the plaintiff's admission that a driver other than the defendant was "to blame." Such an admission, even though in opinion form, is competent evidence under Rule 803(1.2).

(2) Excited Utterance. A statement relating to a startling event or condition made while the declarant was under the stress of excitement caused by the event or condition.

<u>Advisory Commission Comments.</u>
The rule restates Tennessee law.

(3) Then Existing Mental, Emotional, or Physical Condition. A statement of the declarant's then existing state of mind, emotion, sensation, or physical condition (such as intent, plan, motive, design, mental feeling, pain, and bodily health), but not including a statement of memory or belief to prove the fact remembered or believed unless it relates to the execution, revocation, identification, or terms of declarant's will.

<u>Advisory Commission Comments.</u>
This is the state of mind hearsay exception, long recognized by Tennessee courts. Combining the hearsay exception with relevancy principles, declarations of mental state will be admissible to prove mental state at issue or subsequent conduct consistent with that mental state.
Normally such declarations are inadmissible to prove past conduct. Most jurisdictions, however, admit express mental state to prove the prior making or revocation of a will. Tennessee is in the minority by excluding the evidence in wills cases. *Hickey v. Beeler*, 180 Tenn. 31, 171 S.W.2d 277 (1943). The proposal would change the Hickey result and make declarations of mental state competent to prove past conduct in lawsuits concerning wills.
The Commission contemplates that only the declarant's conduct, not some third party's conduct, is provable by this hearsay exception. It views decisions such as *Ford v. State*, 184 Tenn. 443, 201 S.W.2d 539 (1945), as based on faulty analysis.
In addition to declarations of mental state, this proposal also governs declarations of present ("then existing") physical condition. The declaration need not be made to a doctor; any witness who overheard the hearsay statement could repeat it in court under this exception.

(4) Statements for Purposes of Medical Diagnosis and Treatment. Statements made for purposes of medical diagnosis and treatment describing medical history; past or present symptoms, pain, or sensations; or the inception or general character of the cause or external source thereof insofar as reasonably pertinent to diagnosis and treatment.

<u>Advisory Commission Comments.</u>
The proposal continues the Tennessee position of limiting declarations of past physical condition to those made to treating doctors. See *Gulf Refining Co. v. Frazier*, 15 Tenn. App. 662, 688-95 (1932). The declaration must be for both diagnosis and treatment. Declarations of present bodily condition fall within Rule 803(3).
It is important to distinguish declarations of bodily condition, admissible as substantive evidence, from similar declarations used by a physician to support an expert opinion. The latter are not evidence, but rather give weight to the opinion —which is the evidence. T.C.A. § 24-7-114; *State v. Holt*, 222 Tenn. 721, 440 S.W.2d 591 (1969); see Rule 703.

(5) Recorded Recollection. A memorandum or record concerning a matter about which a witness once had knowledge but now has insufficient recollection to enable the witness to testify fully and accurately, shown to have been made or adopted by the witness when the matter was fresh in the witness's memory and to reflect that knowledge correctly. If admitted, the memorandum or record may be read into evidence but may not itself be received as an exhibit unless offered by an adverse party.

<u>**Advisory Commission Comments.**</u>
The proposed rule recognizes the traditional Tennessee hearsay exception for past recollection recorded, but it expands common law in two respects. It allows the admissibility of the contents of a document reflecting past recollection recorded even though the witness has some recollection of the recorded facts but not enough to testify "fully and accurately." Second, it permits the witness to adopt a record made by another not acting under the witness's supervision. The safeguard is the requirement of adoption at the time when the witness could vouch for the document's correctness. The proposal restricts the common law by confining presentation of the document to reading the contents rather than exhibiting the paper to the jury. Tennessee law presently permits the writing to be handed to the jurors and, in civil cases, to be taken to the jury room. T.C.A. § 20-9-510. This change is designed to prevent the jury from giving more weight to this hearsay evidence than would have been given to the declarant's live testimony had the declarant been able to testify from present memory.
But note T.C.A. § 55-10-114(b) and *McBee v. Williams*, 56 Tenn. App. 232, 405 S.W.2d 668 (1966), concerning accident reports. See the Comment to Rule 803(8).

(6) Records of Regularly Conducted Activity. A memorandum, report, record, or data compilation, in any form, of acts, events, conditions, opinions, or diagnoses made at or near the time by or from information transmitted by a person with knowledge and a business duty to record or transmit if kept in the course of a regularly conducted business activity and if it was the regular practice of that business activity to make the memorandum, report, record or data compilation, all as shown by the testimony of the custodian or other qualified witness or by certification that complies with Rule 902(11) or a statute permitting certification, unless the source of information or the method or circumstances of preparation indicate lack of trustworthiness. The term "business" as used in this paragraph includes business, institution, profession, occupation, and calling of every kind, whether or not conducted for profit. [As amended by order filed January 23, 2001, effective July 1, 2001.]

<u>**Advisory Commission Comments.**</u>
This rule essentially is the same as the Uniform Business Records as Evidence Act, T.C.A. § 24-7-111 [repealed]. To avoid interpretive mistakes such as that in *Wheeler v. Cain*, 62 Tenn. App. 126, 459 S.W.2d 618 (1970), the proposal specifically requires that the declarant have "a business duty to record or transmit" information. Without that duty, a business record would lack the trustworthiness necessary to carve out a hearsay exception.

<u>**Advisory Commission Comments [1994].**</u>
Police reports of traffic accidents are inadmissible under T.C.A. § 55-10-114(b) and T.R.Evid. 803(8).

Amended Rule 803(6) in conjunction with new Rule 902(11) eliminates the need to call the custodian of records as a trial witness. Such a procedure has been in effect by statute for medical business records. See T.C.A. §§24-9-101(8) & 68-11-401 et seq.

(7) [Reserved.]

It is doubtful that the absence of a business entry poses a hearsay problem. Consequently, although F.R.Evid. 803(7) contains a purported exception, the Commission found no need for an exception.

(8) Public Records and Reports. Unless the source of information or the method or circumstances of preparation indicate lack of trustworthiness, records, reports, statements, or data compilations in any form of public offices or agencies setting forth the activities of the office or agency or matters observed pursuant to a duty imposed by law as to which matters there was a duty to report, excluding, however, matters observed by police officers and other law enforcement personnel. [As amended by order filed January 25, 1991, effective July 1, 1991.]

The rule admits records of public officials acting under an official duty to report accurately. This is the traditional official records hearsay exception. T.R.C.P. 44; T.C.A. §§ 24-6-105 —107.
Police reports are expressly excluded, just as they are under current law in some instances. See *McBee v. Williams*, 56 Tenn. App. 232, 405 S.W.2d 668 (1966), construing T.C.A. § 55-10-114(b) to exclude accident reports. See also T.C.A. § 55-12-108(b), excluding Department of Safety determinations of fault in automobile accidents.
[Deleted in 1993: As to other statutory modifications and decisional embellishments, see Tennessee Law of Evidence §§ 82-86.]
The Commission borrowed language from subsections (A) and (B) of F.R.Evid. 803(8), but it expressly rejected federal subsection (C) on factual findings from investigations. The term "activities" in proposed subsection (A) is limited to the internal operations of a public office, making this category of official records much like business records of a private organization. The introductory language cautions that sources of information must be trustworthy.

This is a technical correction.

Delete the third paragraph of the comment.

(9) Records of Vital Statistics. Records or data compilations in any form of births, fetal deaths, deaths, marriages, or divorces, if the report was made to a public office pursuant to requirements of law. [As amended by order filed January 25, 1991, effective July 1, 1991, and February 13, 1991, effective July 1, 1991.]

Vital statistics, a particular variety of official records, come in under this exception. Tennessee law is unchanged. T.C.A. § 68-3-101 et seq.

Advisory Commission Comments [1991].
The amendment adds divorce records to the list of vital statistics.

(10) [Reserved.]

Advisory Commission Comments.
Although T.C.A. § 24-6-107 permits a filing officer to certify complete absence of an alleged record in the files, there is no Tennessee authority for making this absence a hearsay exception. Moreover, since the Commission believes that the absence of an entry in a public record is not a hearsay statement, no hearsay exception is needed. F.R.Evid. 803(10) purports to state a hearsay exception.

(11) [Reserved.]

Advisory Commission Comments.
The Commission did not believe records of religious organizations were uniformly reliable enough to satisfy hearsay exception requirements.

(12) Marriage, Baptismal, and Similar Certificates. Statements of fact contained in a certificate that the maker performed a marriage or other ceremony or administered a sacrament made by a member of the clergy, a public official, or another person authorized by the rules or practices of a religious organization or by law to perform the act certified and purporting to have been issued at the time of the act or within a reasonable time thereafter.

Advisory Commission Comments.
This exception is similar to those in Rules 803(8) and (9). Marriage and baptism necessarily involve religious or official participation, and the religious or public record is evidence of the fact of baptism or marriage.

(13) Family Records. Statements of fact concerning personal or family history contained in family Bibles, genealogies, engravings on rings, inscriptions on family portraits, engravings on burial urns, crypts, tombstones, or the like. [As amended by order filed January 25, 1991, effective July 1, 1991.]

Advisory Commission Comments.
While not always trustworthy, family records of the kinds described here may be the only evidence available. In any event, once admitted through this hearsay exception, the facts can be rebutted.

Advisory Commission Comments [1991].
This is a technical amendment.

(14) Records of Documents Affecting an Interest in Property. The record of a document purporting to establish or affect an interest in property as proof of the contents of the original recorded document and its execution and delivery by each person by whom it purports to have been executed if the record is a record of a public office and an applicable statute authorizes the recording of documents of that kind in that office.

Advisory Commission Comments.
This exception is a narrow one. It admits only three facts about a recorded deed, financing statement, or other property instrument: (1) the contents of a certified copy are identical to the filed original, (2) the original was executed, and (3) the original was delivered (if that step is necessary).

(15) [Reserved.]

Advisory Commission Comments.
Statements of "fact" in a warranty deed, trust deed, or security agreement are not trustworthy enough to justify admissibility as truth. Consequently, the Commission rejected the contrary view in F.R.Evid. 803(15).

(16) Statements in Ancient Documents Affecting an Interest in Property. Statements in a document in existence thirty years or more purporting to establish or affect an interest in property, the authenticity of which is established.

Advisory Commission Comments.
If a document —be it a deed, security agreement, or other instrument —affects a property interest, and if it is thirty years old and authentic, the trier of fact may take as true statements within the document. Proposed Rule 901(b) makes thirty years of age one of the requisites for authentication, but the offering lawyer must also establish normal custody and lack of suspicion.
Tennessee decisions treat admissibility of ancient deeds, but the proposed exception updates the law to cover other property instruments. Otherwise, the rule is consistent with present Tennessee law. It departs markedly from F.R.Evid. 803(16) which provides a hearsay exception for any (not just property) documents at least twenty years old.

(17) Market Reports and Commercial Publications. Market quotations, tabulations, lists, directories, or other published compilations, generally used and relied upon by the public or by persons in particular occupations.

Advisory Commission Comments.
Tennessee's Uniform Commercial Code admits commodity market quotations in T.C.A. § 47-2-724. The proposed exception extends the exception to other publications generally relied upon by the public.

(18) [Reserved.]

Advisory Commission Comments.
Learned treatises can be used to impeach an expert but are not themselves admissible to prove the truth of their contents. No good reason exists to permit hearsay to be taken as true just because it is written in books. F.R.Evid. 803(18) is contra.

(19) Reputation Concerning Personal or Family History. Reputation among members of a person's family by blood, adoption, or marriage or among associates or in the community concerning a person's birth, adoption, marriage, divorce, death, legitimacy, relationship by blood, adoption, or marriage, ancestry, or other similar fact of personal or family history.

<u>Advisory Commission Comments.</u>
The rule admits reputation to prove pedigree, and that is the common law and Tennessee position. To introduce an individual's declaration to prove pedigree, see Rule 804(b)(4).
The proposal contains no requirement that the reputation have existed before the controversy developed.

(20) Reputation Concerning Ancient Boundaries. Reputation in a community, arising before the controversy and existing thirty years, as to the boundaries of or customs affecting lands in the community.

<u>Advisory Commission Comments.</u>
The rule mirrors current Tennessee law.

(21) Reputation As to Character. Reputation of a person's character among associates or in the community.

<u>Advisory Commission Comments.</u>
Character evidence primarily involves relevancy issues, but it requires a hearsay exception as well to gain admittance. This hearsay exception is standard.
The exception satisfies the hearsay exclusionary rule, but other evidence principles must be satisfied as well. See Proposed Rules 404, 405, and 408.

(22) Judgment of Previous Conviction. Evidence of a final judgment adjudging a person guilty of a crime punishable by death or imprisonment in excess of one year to prove any fact essential to sustain the judgment, but not including, when offered by the prosecution in a criminal case for purposes other than impeachment, judgments against persons other than the accused. The pendency of an appeal may be shown but does not affect admissibility.

<u>Advisory Commission Comments.</u>
The rule adopts the federal approach admitting felony conviction records to prove underlying facts necessary to the judgment. Tennessee has followed the common law view excluding such evidence. *Smith v. Phillips*, 43 Tenn. App. 364, 309 S.W.2d 382 (1956).
Civil judgments are routinely admitted to bar relitigation on res judicata principles. In limited circumstances, federal constitutional law collaterally estops subsequent prosecutions.
The Commission believed that a jury's finding beyond a reasonable doubt that a serious crime was committed should be admitted in a later civil or criminal trial to prove the underlying facts necessary to the judgment of conviction. Because facts proving minor crimes may not have been developed at trial, the rule would exclude judgments for lesser infractions from this hearsay exception.

(23) Judgment As to Personal or Family History or Boundaries. Judgments as proof of matters of personal or family history or boundaries, which matters were essential to the judgment.

Advisory Commission Comments.
The rule makes civil and criminal judgments admissible to prove boundaries and personal or family history. Reliability is relatively high, and need is great.

(24) [Reserved.]

Advisory Commission Comments.
The proposed rules contain no residual exception such as that in Fed.R.Evid. 803 (24).

(25) Children's Statements. Provided that the circumstances indicate trustworthiness, statements about abuse or neglect made by a child alleged to be the victim of physical, sexual, or psychological abuse or neglect, offered in a civil action concerning issues of dependency and neglect pursuant to Tenn. Code Ann. § 37-1-102(b)(12), issues concerning severe child abuse pursuant to Tenn. Code Ann. § 37-1-102(b)(21), or issues concerning termination of parental rights pursuant to Tenn. Code Ann. § 37-1-147 and Tenn. Code Ann. § 36-1-113, and statements about abuse or neglect made by a child alleged to be the victim of physical, sexual, or psychological abuse offered in a civil trial relating to custody, shared parenting, or visitation. Declarants of age thirteen or older at the time of the hearing must testify unless unavailable as defined by Rule 804(a); otherwise this exception is inapplicable to their extrajudicial statements.

Advisory Commission Comments.
Rule 803(25) is a narrow exception. It applies only if the specified issues are material. Even then it is inapplicable if the minor declarant has reached age thirteen by the time of hearing and is available as a witness but does not testify.

Declarations under this hearsay exception are inadmissible if "circumstances indicate lack of trustworthiness." Courts should carefully consider the motivation of particular minor declarants and also the motivation of some adults to influence children. Also worthy of consideration is the presence or absence of evidence corroborating the hearsay statement. As with all hearsay offered at trial, balancing under Rule 403 is appropriate.

The exception is not limited to juvenile court hearings, although it replaces a portion of T.R.Juv.P. 28(c). This new exception applies, for example, in a circuit court trial concerning the itemized issues. The exception is limited by its terms to civil actions as opposed to criminal prosecutions.

The bench and bar should keep in mind that other exceptions in Rule 803 and 804 may serve to admit children's hearsay declarations. Examples include excited utterances, declarations of mental state, declarations of physical condition, or former testimony. Also, some extrajudicial statements are relevant on a nonhearsay basis.

Certain juvenile proceedings other than adjudicatory hearings admit "reliable hearsay." See T.R.Juv.P. 15(b), 16(a), and 32(f).

Advisory Commission Comment [2003].
Rule 803(25) is amended to extend the children's statements exception to some issues in a divorce action tried in circuit or chancery courts. Note that a condition precedent to admissibility in any court, including juvenile, is that "the circumstances indicate trustworthiness" of the hearsay. Another change is to incorporate revisions in statutory citations.

(26) Prior Inconsistent Statements of a Testifying Witness. A statement otherwise admissible under Rule 613(b) if all of the following conditions are satisfied:

(A) The declarant must testify at the trial or hearing and be subject to cross-examination concerning the statement.

(B) The statement must be an audio or video recorded statement, a written statement signed by the witness, or a statement given under oath.

(C) The judge must conduct a hearing outside the presence of the jury to determine by a preponderance of the evidence that the prior statement was made under circumstances indicating trustworthiness. [As amended by order filed January 28, 1993, and effective July 1, 1993; by order filed January 31, 2003, and effective July 1, 2003; and by order filed January 8, 2009, and effective July 1, 2009.]

Advisory Commission Comment [2009].

Subsection (26) alters Tennessee law by permitting some prior inconsistent statements to be treated as substantive evidence. Many other jurisdictions have adopted this approach to address circumstances where witnesses suddenly claim a lack of memory in light of external threats of violence which cannot be directly attributed to a party, for example. This rule incorporates several safeguards to assure that the prior inconsistent statements are both reliable and authentic.

To be considered as substantive evidence the statement must first meet the traditional conditions of admissibility which include the procedural aspects of inconsistent statements as addressed in Rule 61 3. This reference also makes clear that only prior inconsistent statements, and not consistent statements, are within the ambit of this rule.

Assuming the inconsistent statement is otherwise admissible to impeach the testifying witness, the party may then seek to have the statement treated as substantive evidence by complying with the rule's other requirements. Other rules address authenticity of documents and recordings which clearly apply here. See e.g. Rule 1001. However, this rule contains additional express requirements regarding the form of the prior statement so that the jury is assured that the statement contains the actual "words" of the witness on a prior occasion. For example the prior statement must be an audio or video recorded statement. A "police report" or insurance investigator's "transcription" of the recorded statement would not qualify since it is not literally the witness's own words contained on audio or video media.

If not recorded, the prior statement can be in written form (created by the witness or by another) but then must be signed by the witness. The commission intends that the "signed" requirement must be equated with an actual signature as opposed to some email document which happens to have the witness's name on the address. Finally, the rule permits a prior statement to be treated as substantive evidence if given under oath.

The rule requires that the party seeking to have the statement treated as substantive evidence request a hearing out of the presence of the jury to satisfy the judge "by a preponderance of the evidence that the prior statement was made under circumstances indicating trustworthiness." This is to prevent fraud such as where a parent tape records a child after training the child to say "bad things" about the other parent in anticipation of a custody dispute. Rules 703 (Bases of Opinion Testimony by Experts) and 803(6) (Records of Regularly Conducted Activity) contain similar judicial gate-keeping requirements.

(a) Definition of Unavailability - "Unavailability of a witness" includes situations in which the declarant:

(1) is exempted by ruling of the court on the grounds of privilege from testifying concerning the subject matter of the declarant's statement; or

(2) persists in refusing to testify concerning the subject matter of the declarant's statement despite an order of the court to do so; or

(3) demonstrates a lack of memory of the subject matter of the declarant's statement; or

(4) is unable to be present or to testify at the hearing because of the declarant's death or then existing physical or mental illness or infirmity; or

(5) is absent from the hearing and the proponent of a statement has been unable to procure the declarant's attendance by process; or

(6) for depositions in civil actions only, is at a greater distance than 100 miles from the place of trial or hearing.

A declarant is not unavailable as a witness if exemption, refusal, claim of lack of memory, inability, or absence is due to the procurement or wrongdoing of the proponent of a statement for the purpose of preventing the witness from attending or testifying.

<u>Advisory Commission Comments.</u>
These grounds for unavailability are familiar to Tennessee practitioners. The fourth and fifth – death, illness, and impossibility of subpoena – are typically the reasons a declarant is unavailable to testify. The first two bases found acceptance by the Supreme Court in *Breeden v. Independent Fire Ins. Co.*, 530 S.W.2d 769 (Tenn. 1975).

<u>Advisory Commission Comments [1994].</u>
The third ground for unavailability is new. Memory lapse, if demonstrated to the trial judge under Rule 104(a), is enough to get the contents of recorded recollection read to the jury, and the same condition should be enough to get cross-examining sworn former testimony before the jury. The new provision also applies to declarations against interest and individual declarations of pedigree.

<u>Advisory Commission Comments [1997].</u>
This amendment conforms Tenn.R.Civ.P. 32 and Tenn.R.Evid. 804. If the former testimony is a deposition, an additional ground of unavailability is a distance of over 100 miles between the deponent and the courthouse.

<u>Advisory Commission Comments [1998].</u>
The amendment to Rule 804(a) is technical.

<u>Advisory Commission Comment [2003].</u>
Paragraph (a)(6) is amended to restrict the 100 mile unavailability ground to depositions in civil, not criminal, trials.

(b) Hearsay Exceptions - The following are not excluded by the hearsay rule if the declarant is unavailable as a witness:

(1) *Former Testimony.* Testimony given as a witness at another hearing of the same or a different proceeding or in a deposition taken in compliance with law in the course of the same or another proceeding, if the party against whom the testimony is now offered had both an opportunity and a similar motive to develop the testimony by direct, cross, or redirect examination.

Advisory Commission Comments.
The rule makes admissible former testimony even though one of the present parties was not at the earlier hearing, but only if the former testimony is offered against the party common to both hearings. In summary, no mutuality of parties is required, such as requirement having been abolished in *State v. Causby*, 706 S.W.2d 628 (Tenn. 1986).

The rule covers depositions as well as trial and preliminary hearing transcripts. Amended T.R.C.P. 32.01 contains the same principle of admissibility for depositions.

By specifically requiring "both an opportunity and a similar motive,"this proposed rule is designed to avoid the holdings of *Lloyd v. American Export Lines, Inc.*, 580 F.2d 1179 (3d Cir. 1978), and *Clay v. Johns-Manville Sales Corp.*, 722 F.2d 1289 (6th Cir. 1983).

(2) *Statement Under Belief of Impending Death.* In a prosecution for homicide or in a civil action or proceeding, a statement made by a declarant while believing that the declarant's death was imminent and concerning the cause or circumstances of what the declarant believed to be impending death.

Advisory Commission Comments.
The rule retains Tennessee's common law limitations. The trial must be for homicide of the declarant, and the declaration is limited to circumstances surrounding the declarant's death. Obviously with this restricted exception, the ground for declarant's unavailability invariably will be death.

Advisory Commission Comments [2009].
The revised language makes admissible a dying declaration even though the declarant is not the victim of the homicide being prosecuted. The exception would apply, for example, where there were multiple victims but the prosecutions were severed. The revision also admits dying declarations in civil cases where relevant and material.

(3) *Statement Against Interest.* A statement which was at the time of its making so far contrary to the declarant's pecuniary or proprietary interest, or so far tended to subject the declarant to civil or criminal liability or to render invalid a claim by the declarant against another, that a reasonable person in the declarant's position would not have made the statement unless believing it to be true.

Advisory Commission Comments.
This rule follows modern Tennessee law by admitting declarations against penal interest as well as those against pecuniary or proprietary interest. *Breeden v. Independent Fire Ins. Co.*, 530 S.W.2d 769 (Tenn. 1975); *Smith v. State,* 587 S.W.2d 659 (Tenn. 1979). The proposal eliminates the condition espoused by Smith that declarations against penal interest offered by the accused in a criminal prosecution must be corroborated.

(4) *Statement of Personal and Family History.* A statement made before the controversy arose (A) concerning declarant's own birth, adoption, marriage, divorce, or legitimacy; relationship by blood, adoption, or marriage; ancestry; or other similar fact of personal or family history; even though the declarant had no means of acquiring personal knowledge of the matter asserted; or (B) concerning the foregoing matters, and death also, of another person if the declarant was related to the other by blood, adoption, or marriage or was so intimately associated with the other's family as to be likely to have accurate information concerning the matter declared.

Advisory Commission Comments.
When pedigree evidence is an individual's extrajudicial declaration rather than the community consensus, the declarant must be unavailable and must have spoken or written "before the controversy arose." The rule reflects Tennessee common law.

(5) *[Reserved.]*

Advisory Commission Comments.
There is no residual exception even where declarants are unavailable. Occasionally, however, constitutional considerations require a tribunal permit the accused in a criminal case to introduce trustworthy hearsay not falling within a traditional exception. See *Chambers v. Mississippi*, 410 U.S. 284, 93 S. Ct. 1038, 35 L. Ed. 2d 297 (1973). See also F.R.Evid. 804(b)(5).

(6) *Forfeiture by Wrongdoing.* A statement offered against a party that has engaged in wrongdoing that was intended to and did procure the unavailability of the declarant as a witness.

[As amended by order entered December 20, 1994, effective July 1, 1994; by order effective July 1, 1997; and by order effective July 1, 1998; as added by order entered January 26, 1999, effective July 1, 1999; by order entered January 31, 2003, effective July 1, 2003; and by order entered January 8, 2009, effective July 1, 2009.]

Advisory Commission Comments [1999].
Rule 804(b)(6) adds a new hearsay exception. It seems only fair to let a party offer any extrajudicial statements of declarants whose unavailability was procured by the opponent.

RULE 805: HEARSAY WITHIN HEARSAY.

Hearsay within hearsay is not excluded under the hearsay rule if each part of the combined statements conforms with an exception to the hearsay rule provided in these rules or otherwise by law.

The rule provides that out-of-court statement containing several levels of hearsay and multiple declarants is nonetheless admissible if a hearsay exception applies to each declarant's statement. Also, while not covered here, a particular declarant's statement in the chain may be admissible as nonhearsay.

Often hospital records contain a nurse's notation that a patient said something to the nurse. In that instance a court must deal with two hearsay declarations. The nurse's notation is admissible as a business record to the extent of showing what words were spoken. The patient's statement may then be admissible under the admissions exception to the declarations of physical condition exception.

RULE 806: ATTACKING AND SUPPORTING CREDIBILITY OF DECLARANT.

When a hearsay statement has been admitted in evidence, the credibility of the declarant may be attacked and, if attacked, may be supported by any evidence which would be admissible for those purposes if declarant had testified as a witness. Evidence of a statement or conduct by the declarant at any time, inconsistent with the declarant's hearsay statement, is not subject to any requirement that the declarant may have been afforded an opportunity to deny or explain. If the party against whom a hearsay statement has been admitted calls the declarant as a witness, the party is entitled to examine the declarant on the statement as if under cross-examination.

The rule makes clear that hearsay declarants are subject to impeachment to the same extent as trial witnesses. if the method of impeachment is by prior inconsistent statement, such statement is not excluded for failure to provide the declarant an opportunity to explain. See Rule 613(b).

Article IX. Authentication

RULE 901: REQUIREMENT OF AUTHENTICATION OR IDENTIFICATION.

(a) General Provision - The requirement of authentication or identification as a condition precedent to admissibility is satisfied by evidence sufficient to the court to support a finding by the trier of fact that the matter in question is what its proponent claims.

(b) Illustrations - By way of illustration only, and not by way of limitation, the following are examples of authentication or identification conforming with the requirements of this rule:

(1) *Testimony of Witness With Knowledge.* Testimony that a matter is what it is claimed to be.

(2) *Nonexpert Opinion on Handwriting.* Nonexpert opinion as to the genuineness of handwriting, based upon familiarity not acquired for purposes of the litigation.

(3) *Comparison by Trier of Fact or Expert Witness.* Comparison by trier of fact or by expert witnesses with specimens which have been authenticated.

(4) *Distinctive Characteristics and the Like.* Appearance, contents, substance, internal patterns, or other distinctive characteristics, taken in conjunction with circumstances.

(5) *Voice Identification.* Identification of a voice, whether heard firsthand or through mechanical or electronic transmission or recording, by opinion based upon hearing the voice at any time under circumstances connecting it with the alleged speaker.

(6) *Telephone Conversations.* Telephone conversations, by evidence that a call was made to the number assigned at the time by a telephone company to a particular person or business if (A), in the case of a person, circumstances including self-identification show the person answering to be the one called or (B), in the case of the business, the call was made to a place of business and the conversation related to business reasonably transacted over the telephone.

(7) *Public Records or Reports.* Evidence that a writing authorized by law to be recorded or filed and in fact recorded or filed in a public office (or a purported public record, report, statement, or data compilation in any form) is from the public office where items of this nature are kept.

(8) *Ancient Documents or Data Compilation.* Evidence that a document or data compilation in any form (A) is in such condition as to create no suspicion concerning its authenticity, (B) was in a place where, if authentic, it would likely be, and (C) has been in existence thirty years or more at the time it is offered.

(9) *Process or System.* Evidence describing a process or system used to produce a result and showing that the process or system produces an accurate result.

(10) *Methods Provided by Statute or Rule.* Any method of authentication or identification provided by Act of Congress or the Tennessee Legislature or by other rules prescribed by the Tennessee Supreme Court.

Advisory Commission Comments.

Section (a) makes the trial judge arbiter of authentication issues, as does the common law.

Subsection (b)(3) lets the trier of fact or an expert compare exemplars and questioned documents. The proposed draft corrects the mistake in *Franklin v. Franklin*, 90 Tenn. 44, 16 S.W. 557 (1891), where the Supreme Court construed T.C.A. § 24-7-108 to disallow purported forger's exemplar. See *Amburn v. State*, 553 S.W.2d 922 (Tenn. Crim. App. 1977), criticizing Franklin.

Subsection (b)(4) simply makes common sense. Without drawing the boundaries of practical possibilities, the rule allows proof to the court of a myriad of distinctive characteristics that may convince the judge that a questioned document is authentic enough to let the jury consider it.

Subsection (b)(9) treats authentication of computer documents. All that the lawyer need do is introduce evidence satisfying the court that the computer system produces accurate information.

Extrinsic evidence of authenticity as a condition precedent to admissibility is not required as to the following:

(1) Domestic Public Documents Under Seal - A document bearing a seal purporting to be that of the State of Tennessee, the United States (or of any other state, district, commonwealth, territory, or insular possession thereof, or the Panama Canal Zone, or the Trust Territory of the Pacific Islands), or of a political subdivision, department, office, or agency thereof, and a signature purporting to be an attestation or execution.

(2) Domestic Public Documents Not Under Seal - A document purporting to bear the signature in the official capacity of an officer or employee of any entity included in paragraph (1) having no seal, if a public officer having a seal and having official duties in the district or political subdivision of the officer or employee certifies under seal that the signer has the official capacity and that the signature is genuine.

(3) Foreign Public Documents - A document purporting to be executed or attested in an official capacity by a person authorized by the laws of a foreign country to make execution or attestation, accompanied by a final certification as to the genuineness of the signature and official position (A) of the executing or attesting person or (B) of any foreign official whose certificate of genuineness of signature and official position relates to the execution or attestation or is in a chain of certificates of genuineness of signature and official position relating to the execution or attestation. A final certification may be made by a secretary of embassy or legation, consul general, consul, vice consul, or consular agent of the United States, or a diplomatic or consular official of the foreign country assigned or accredited to the United States. If reasonable opportunity has been given to all parties to investigate the authenticity and accuracy of official documents, the court may for good cause shown order that they be treated as presumptively authentic without final certification or permit them to be evidenced by an attested summary with or without final certification.

(4) Certified Copies of Public Records - A copy of an official record or report or entry therein, or of a document authorized by law to be recorded or filed and actually recorded or filed in a public office (including data compilations in any form), certified as correct by the custodian or other person authorized to make the certification, by certificate complying with paragraph (1), (2), or (3) of this rule or complying with any Act of Congress or the Tennessee Legislature or rule prescribed by the Tennessee Supreme Court.

(5) Official Publications - Books, pamphlets, or other publications purporting to be issued by public authority.

(6) Newspapers and Periodicals - Printed material purporting to be newspapers and periodicals.

(7) Trade Inscriptions and the Like - Inscriptions, sign, tags, or labels purporting to have been affixed in the course of business and indicating ownership, control or origin.

(8) Acknowledged Documents - Documents accompanied by a certificate of acknowledgment executed in the manner provided by law by a notary public or other officer authorized by law to take acknowledgments.

(9) Commercial Paper and Related Documents - Commercial paper, including all signatures, and related documents to the extent provided by general commercial law.

(10) Presumptions Under Acts of Congress or the Legislature - Any signature, document, or other matter declared by Act of Congress or the Tennessee Legislature to be presumptively or prima facie authentic.

(11) Certified Records of Regularly Conducted Activity - The original or a duplicate of a domestic record of regularly conducted activity that would be admissible under Rule 803(6) if accompanied by an affidavit of its custodian or other qualified person certifying that the record:

(A) was made at or near the time of the occurrence of the matters set forth by, or from information transmitted by, a person with knowledge of and a business duty to record or transmit those matters;

(B) was kept in the course of the regularly conducted activity; and

(C) was made by the regularly conducted activity as a regular practice.

A party intending to offer a record into evidence under this paragraph must provide written notice of that intention to all adverse parties, and must make the record and declaration available for inspection sufficiently in advance of their offer into evidence to provide an adverse party with a fair opportunity to challenge them.

[As amended by order entered January 23, 2001, effective July 1, 2001; and by order entered January 31, 2003, effective July 1, 2003.]

Advisory Commission Comments.
This rule lists documents that do not require authenticating evidence as a foundation to admissibility.

Part (9) refers to Tennessee's version of the Uniform Commercial Code, T.C.A. § 47-1-101 et seq. See in particular T.C.A. § 47-3-307, concerning signatures on commercial paper.

Advisory Commission Comments [2001].
Read in conjunction with Rule 803(6), new Rule 902(11) allows affidavits by custodians to establish the foundation for business records. The custodian need not attend trial as a witness.

Advisory Commission Comment [2003].
The business duty element of a foundation for the business records hearsay exception is inserted in Rule 902(11)(A) to conform to Rule 803(6).

RULE 903: SUBSCRIBING WITNESSES' TESTIMONY.

The testimony of a subscribing witness is not necessary to authenticate a writing unless required by statute.

[As amended by ordered filed December 14, 2009, effective July 1, 2010..]

Advisory Commission Comments.
In will contests, T.C.A. § 32-4-105 requires calling subscribing witnesses to a will.

Advisory Commission Comment [2010].
The title of the rule is changed to reflect reality. A Tennessee statute does not necessitate testimony of all living witnesses in a will contest "if to be found." T.C.A. § 32-4-105.

Article X. Contents of Writings, Recordings, and Photographs

RULE 1001: DEFINITIONS.

For purposes of this article the following definitions are applicable:

(1) Writings and Recordings - "Writings" and "recordings" consist of letters, words, numbers, sounds, or their equivalent, set down by handwriting, typewriting, printing, photostating, photographing, magnetic impulse, mechanical or electronic recording, or other form of data compilation.

(2) Photographs - "Photographs" include still photographs, x-ray films, video tapes, and motion pictures.

(3) Original - An "original" of a writing or recording is the writing or recording itself or any counterpart intended to have the same effect by a person executing or issuing it. An "original" of a photograph includes the negative or any print. If data are stored in a computer or similar device, any printout or other output readable by sight and shown to reflect the data accurately is an "original."

(4) Duplicate - A "duplicate" is a copy produced by the same impression as the original, or from the same matrix, or by means of photography, including enlargements and miniatures, or by mechanical or electronic re-recording, or by chemical reproduction, or by other equivalent techniques which accurately reproduce the original.

<u>Advisory Commission Comments.</u>

Tennessee's existing best evidence rule, also known as the original document rule, undergoes expansion in proposed Rules 1001 and 1003. As a practical matter, the most significant provision is the definition of "duplicate" in Rule 1001(4), which encompasses the copies familiar to all lawyers with copying machines. Support for admissibility can be found in *Bolton v. State*, 617 S.W.2d 909 (Tenn. Crim. App. 1981). The copy usually would be admissible on an equal plane with an "original" under Rule 1003.

<u>Advisory Commission Comments [1999].</u>

The Commission believes that the language in subsection (1) defining "writings and recordings" is sufficiently broad to cover electronic imaging, a process by which documents are read into a computer by a scanner for electronic storage. That is a "form of data compilation." Moreover, the General Assembly reenacted the Uniform Photographic Copies of Business and Public Records as Evidence Act, T.C.A. § 24-7-119, effective April 29, 1998.

RULE 1002: REQUIREMENT OF ORIGINAL.

To prove the content of a writing, recording, or photograph, the original writing, recording, or photograph is required, except as otherwise provided in these rules or by Act of Congress or the Tennessee Legislature.

<u>Advisory Commission Comments.</u>

This rule states the traditional preference for an "original," but Rules 1001(4) and 1003 should be consulted. Usually the court will admit machine copies.

A duplicate is admissible to the same extent as an original unless a genuine question is raised as to the authenticity of the original.

Advisory Commission Comments.
This rule is the key to an understanding of the best evidence rule as the Commission contemplates it. Normally business people and lawyers accept machine copies as authentic. There is no reason why courts should not take the same approach in most instances. See Rule 1001(4) for the definition of "duplicate."

The original is not required, and other evidence of a writing, recording, or photograph is admissible if:
(1) Originals Lost or Destroyed - All originals are lost or destroyed, unless the proponent lost or destroyed them in bad faith; or
(2) Original Not Obtainable - No original can be obtained by any available judicial process or procedure; or
(3) Original in Possession of Opponent - At a time when an original was under the control of the party against whom offered, that party was put on notice by the pleadings or otherwise that the contents would be a subject of proof at the hearing but does not produce the original at the hearing; or
(4) Collateral Matters - The writing, recording, or photograph is not closely related to a controlling issue.

Advisory Commission Comments.
In the rare situation where neither an "original" nor a "duplicate" is offered, this rule enumerates the common law excuses for failure to present the best evidence.

The contents of an official record, or of a document authorized to be recorded or filed and actually recorded or filed, including data compilations in any form, if otherwise admissible may be proved by copy certified as correct in accordance with Rule 902 or testified to be correct by a witness who has compared it with the original. If a copy which compiles with the foregoing cannot be obtained by the exercise of reasonable diligence, then other evidence of the contents may be given.

Advisory Commission Comments.
Copies of public records are the best evidence if certified or otherwise authenticated under the rule.

The contents of voluminous writings, recordings, or photographs which cannot conveniently be examined in court may be presented in the form of a chart, summary or calculation. The originals or duplicates shall be made available for examination or copying, or both, by other parties at reasonable times and places. The court may order that they be produced in court.

<u>**Advisory Commission Comments.**</u>
Summaries of the contents of voluminous documents have long been admissible in Tennessee. State ex rel. *Stewart v. Follis*, 140 Tenn. 513, 521, 205 S.W. 444 (1918).

RULE 1007: TESTIMONY OR WRITTEN ADMISSION OF PARTY.

Contents of writings, recordings, or photographs may be proved by the testimony, deposition, or written admission of the party against whom offered, without accounting for nonproduction of the original.

<u>**Advisory Commission Comments.**</u>
This rule dispenses with the original document requirement in the circumstances described. Note that the proposed rule requires an unsworn statement of the contents of a document to be in writing.

RULE 1008: FUNCTIONS OF COURT AND JURY.

When the admissibility of other evidence of contents of writings, recordings, or photographs under these rules depends upon the fulfillment of a condition of fact, the question of whether the condition has been fulfilled is ordinarily for the court to determine in accordance with the provisions of Rule 104. When an issue is raised as to (a) whether the asserted writing, recording, or photograph ever existed, or (b) whether another writing, recording, or photograph produced at the trial is the original, or (c) whether other evidence of contents correctly reflects the contents, the issue is for the trier of fact to determine as in the case of other issues of fact.

<u>**Advisory Commission Comments.**</u>
Division of responsibility between judge and jury is similar to the traditional provisions of Rule 104.